First published 2011
Copyright © 2011 by Tony Hibbert
ISBN   978-1-907741-02-9

Design: Philip Gray
Typeface: Bembo
Print: SS Media Ltd

Published by Fineleaf Editions, 2011
Moss Cottage, Pontshill, Ross-on-Wye HR9 5TB
www.fineleaf.co.uk   books@fineleaf.co.uk

British Library Cataloguing in Publication Data
A catalogue record for this book is available from the British Library.

Fresh flowers for M'Lady

Tony Hibbert

Fineleaf

PUBLISHED BY FINELEAF, ROSS-ON-WYE
www.fineleaf.co.uk

Acknowledgements

I am very grateful for the advice and assistance given by Philip Gray of Fineleaf Publishing. Thanks to my wife, Mair, for her valuable opinion and considerable help with the research. A special thanks to Brecknock Museum and Art Gallery, in particular to my sister, Patti Harries, and the work of the late Canon Josiah Jones Davies of Trecastle, one time Honorary Curator of Brecknock Museum. Canon Davies's research and notes (some published in *Museum News* in the *Brecon and Radnor Express*) proved invaluable in verifying stories and facts. My mother, Getta Hibbert, who at the age of ninety-five was able to relate and confirm many anecdotes about Constantine Hibbert (her father-in-law) and information about Craig-y-Nos Castle as a TB Hospital. Of course a huge debt to Constantine Hibbert, my grandfather, who had the foresight to retain so many photographs, postcards, newspaper cuttings, and memorabilia most of them in excess of 120 years old. Many of the postcards were written in French or Italian and these were kindly translated into English by a family friend, Signora Alessia Ianotta.

Tony Hibbert, 2011

Contents

Foreword

CRAIG-Y-NOS, in Powys, Mid Wales, is a very special place. I had the privilege of being born there in 1943, and spending a happy childhood in this area of outstanding natural beauty.

It is a small village steeped in history, mainly associated with the 'castle'. From 1878 to 1919 this was the home of Adela Juana Maria Patti, or Adelina Patti as she was known throughout the world. She was described by Verdi as 'an artist by nature, so perfect that perhaps there has never been her equal'. For forty years she was Craig-y-Nos, providing employment for the local community and unfailing in her work for charity throughout the Swansea Valley.

Craig-y-Nos, and particularly the neighbouring village of Penwyllt, played a large part in the Industrial Revolution, producing raw materials for the nineteenth century industries of the Swansea Valley and beyond.

On the mountainside overlooking Craig-y-Nos Castle is Dan-yr-ogof Caves, discovered in 1912, and opened to the public between the two world wars. After a period of closure, with further discoveries and redevelopment, the caves were again opened to the public in 1964. It is now one of the leading tourist attractions in Wales.

My grandfather, Constantine Hibbert, was employed at Craig-y-Nos Castle for over 44 years - 30 years as head gardener to Adelina Patti. His close working relationship with Patti and Nicolini, her second husband, and in later years with Cederström, her third husband, helped to develop the castle buildings and grounds into a wonderful home for the world famous diva.

Before arriving at Craig-y-Nos my grandfather was employed at the Duke of Devonshire's Chatsworth House in Derbyshire. At the age of twenty-five he married Welsh-speaking Gwen Potter, whose grandfather William Morgan, son of the Garth, Abercrave, had married Anne Watkins of Gwarscwd - both families having a great influence in shaping the social and economic development of the upper Swansea Valley.

Much has been written about the life and international success of Madam Patti. She was the 'superstar of opera' of the late nineteenth century. My story is a very personal one, with a great deal of sentiment. It is the story of the influence this great lady and the castle had on generations of my family, and many other families in the area.

I feel rather sad that Craig-y-Nos Castle, and its once magnificent grounds, have not been preserved in their original state as a legacy to one of the greatest opera stars of the nineteenth century. Thankfully the beautiful theatre is still intact, but for how long? It is a Grade 1 Listed Building, but is reported to be in a state of disrepair and in need of complete renovation: it appears on the Theatre Buildings At Risk (TABR) list for 2010. The Theatre Trust commented:

This is one of the most important private theatres in Britain, and deserves exceptional effort to see it restored and brought back to fuller use.

I hope money can be found to restore it to its original splendour. Patti deserves it for the immense contribution she made during her lifetime to enhance the quality of life of the people of Craig-y-Nos and surrounding areas.

The original castle grounds, as laid out by Patti, were described in the press of 1891 as 'an incredible place to behold: lakes teeming with fish, manicured lawns and paths, and magnificent trees and rhododendrons.' Today, a large area of the grounds are under the care of Brecon Beacons National Park Authority.

My story starts around the beginning of the nineteenth century and recalls some of the events that shaped the community of the upper reaches of the Swansea Valley, over two centuries. The title of the book is taken from the script of a radio play, *Queen of Song,* which was transmitted by BBC Radio on 23rd September 1953. The line was spoken by the actor Eric Lugg, playing the part of Constantine Hibbert.

Tony Hibbert
2011

One

THE UPPER SWANSEA VALLEY

The early days of the Industrial Revolution seem a logical place to start my journey through the 200 years or so of association my family has had with Craig-y-Nos. Prior to this period, Craig-y-Nos and the surrounding areas consisted mainly of forests, landowners and tenant farmers.

The early eighteenth century saw the development of the smelting works at Ynyscedwyn, although the discovery of a piece of iron, date stamped 1612, suggests evidence of similar workings on this site. Large deposits of iron ore had been discovered here, and the nearby copper works in Landore had become a major British industry by 1778.

The first commercial coal seam was in the area close to the Castle Hotel in Caerlan with the coal being carried on horseback to Ystradgynlais. This seam was bought by a mining engineer, Edward Martin, and his son-in-law and the level was known as Gwaith Davies-Martin. Further coal seams around Abercrave and large limestone deposits on the Cribarth mountain, Craig-y-Nos, meant the revolution had really started.

Around 1830 David Thomas of Ynyscedwyn Iron Works developed the process of smelting iron by burning anthracite coal with limestone, thus eliminating the use of foundry coke. The demand for anthracite coal and limestone became insatiable. David Thomas was born in Cadoxton, Neath, in 1791 and started work in Neath Abbey Ironworks when he was seventeen years of age. He was appointed Superintendent of Ynyscedwyn Ironworks, Ystradgynlais, in 1817 at the age of twenty-six. In 1839 he took his expertise to Pennsylvania, USA and in 1854 founded the Thomas Iron Company which became the largest producer of anthracite pig iron in the USA. He is remembered as David 'Papa' Thomas, the father of the

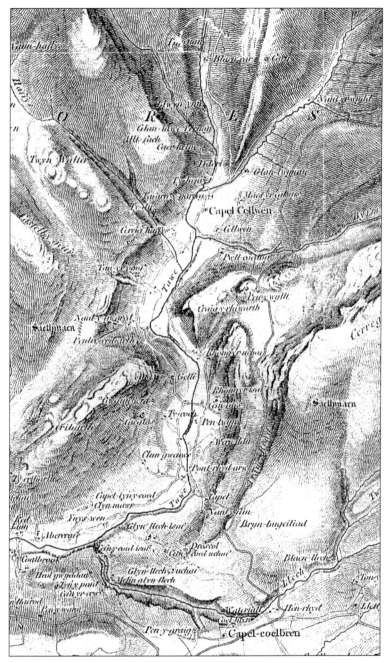

The area (map centre) prior to the building of Craig-y-Nos Castle
Extract from Ordnance Survey First Edition 1 inch to 1 mile map 1831

American Iron Industry. Samuel Lewis in his 1849 Publication, *A Topographical Dictionary of Wales*, wrote about Yniscedwyn:

These extensive works comprise seven blast furnaces for smelting the ore, air furnaces and cupolas for converting the pig-iron into castings, with fineries for making the refined metal used by the tin manufacturers. The furnaces are blown by a large steam engine, made by the Neath Abbey Iron Company, as well as by a powerful machine erected in 1828, from designs by Mr Brunton of London, and worked by a water-wheel of large diameter. The iron ore, limestone and coal used are all procured in the Parish.

In 1798 Parliament approved the construction of a canal to convey the raw materials to Swansea with barges carrying up to 20 tons, with 36 locks compensating for the drop of 300 feet in water level. One of the proprietors of the canal was Daniel Harpur and in 1801 he moved to Abercrave, building Abercrave Mansion near the old Abercrave Farm. He and William Shaxby ran the British Coal and Iron Company, developing the Lefel Fawr Mine and the Abercrave Iron Works.

The British Coal and Iron Company started mining coal from Mynydd-Y-Drum, the Drum Mountain. The coal was transported by tram to Pwll Dover and over the river bridge along further tram lines to the canal terminus at Hen Noyadd. Another tram line from the Cribarth mountain brought the limestone to the terminus.

The blood running through my veins is a mixture of good Welsh farming stock, some of whom developed good civil engineering and business skills in the minerals industry, and two English settlers from Derbyshire and Sussex, who also had a keen interest in the land: one was a gardener and one a warrener/gamekeeper.

Major links in my paternal family tree were the two old established families, the Morgans of Garth Farm, Abercrave, who supported the church, and the Watkins family of Gwarscwd, Abercrave, who were staunch non-conformists, having moved

Hibbert Archives

Penwyllt Brickworks opened circa 1863

Remains of Penwyllt limestone kilns - 2010

Hibbert Archives

from Carmarthenshire to Abercrave. These families were to combine by marriage and have an immense influence on industry, farming and business in the area.

Around 1801, a self taught engineer William Watkins, who had some education at Maes-y-fron Sunday School, and was my great great great grandfather and son of Thomas Watkins of Gwarscwd, impressed Shaxby and Harpur, when he developed the Lefel Fawr mine adjacent to the Swansea Canal. He tunnelled one mile into the hillside without using explosives, shattering the rock by harnessing the expansion produced when lime was slaked with water. Harpur and Shaxby built a new stone bridge, Pont-y-Yard Bridge, over the Tawe river, which was originally intended as an aqueduct to link the Lefel Fawr mine with the Swansea Canal at Hen Noyadd dock. Unfortunately the gradients and the hardness of the local rock meant the canal extension was never completed and coal was transported to the canal by horse drawn tramway. The storage area for coal, the yard, was in an area now crossed by the A4067. This became the hub of coal distribution for many years to come. Watkins also developed methods of using waterpower and the lie of the land to haul coal and limestone to the head of the Swansea Canal. William Shaxby had an adopted daughter, Rachel, née Jones, who very quickly became Mrs William Watkins in 1809.

In the early 1800s copper ore was found in the valley near the Haffes River, Glyntawe, and clay for making pottery near Pen-y-cae. Both proved difficult and expensive to mine and did not succeed. However another two industries, quarrying of rottenstone on the Cribarth at Craig-y-Nos and the manufacture of silica bricks at Penwyllt, both developed by John Christie, were successful. Christie also developed limestone kilns at Penwyllt and built tramroads to transport the limestone. John Christie was a wealthy Scottish-born London indigo merchant whose wealth had enabled him to buy the Crown Allotment of the Great Forest of Brecon. He had built a model farm at Cnewr, on the outskirts of Cray, and his intention was to transport limestone along tramroads from Penwyllt to Cnewr, and eventually to the farms of the Usk valley, to be used for soil improvement. In addition to its importance

Hibbert Archives

Remains of Penwyllt Silica Brickworks - 2010

Cribarth Mountain

Crown Copyright : Royal Commission on the
Ancient and Historical Monuments of Wales

in the iron making industries, burnt lime was used extensively in agriculture as a 'manure' on the heavy soils to make them more open and improve drainage. Christie had laid down a tramroad to transport the limestone to the farms in the heart of Brecknockshire. Samuel Lewis wrote:

> *Christie's tramway, constructed for the purpose of conveying produce to the heart of the county, passes along the sides of the mountains, and through the glens that intersect them near Devynock, to the River Usk.*

Christie quickly overstretched his finances, and finally went bankrupt. His assets were taken over by Joseph Claypon. Initially Claypon did not show a great interest in the business he had acquired and leased the Brecon Forest Tramroad, limekilns, cottages, stables and 70 acres of land to London timber merchants Arnott and Mercer. In 1828 they in turn sub-leased the business to William Watkins, William Powell and David Jeffreys who formed the Brecon Forest Tramroad Company. They concentrated on developing the lime kilns at Penwyllt.

Two years later Arnott and Mercer went bankrupt. The lease reverted direct to Claypon. The Brecon Forest Tramroad Company transported other goods as well as lime between the Castell Du Wharf, Defynnog and the Bristol Channel ports via the Swansea Canal. The Brecon Forest Tramroad Company was wound up in 1840 and Claypon resumed direct control of the limeworks and tramroad until 1857 when a new lease was granted to David Jeffries. Claypon died in 1859 and the whole of the ownership of the Crown Allotment including the tramroad was bought by George Edwards of Bristol.

By 1863 John Dickson was building the Neath and Brecon Railway and eventually bought the limestone quarry. After years of legal wrangling between the Crown appointed trustees and James Dickson, who was a relative of John Dickson, Adelina Patti acquired the limestone works and quarries in Penwyllt. In 1888 she leased them to John Jebb, who operated them as The Penwyllt Lime and Limestone Company.

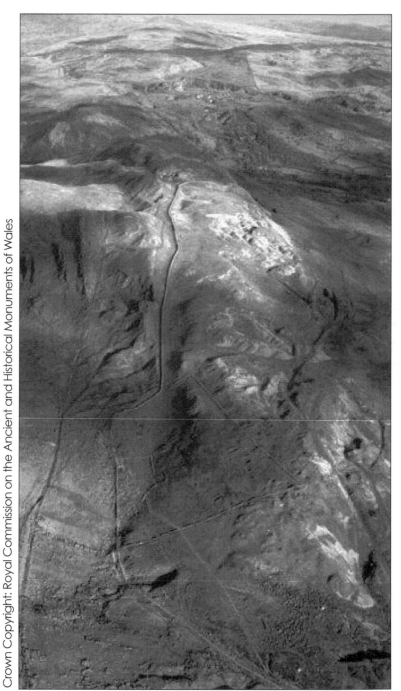

Crown Copyright: Royal Commission on the Ancient and Historical Monuments of Wales

Rottenstone tramroad Cribarth Mountain

Between 1794 and 1890 there were around 30 limestone quarries on the Cribarth mountain. To access the Swansea Canal near Hen Noyadd, 10 miles of horse-drawn tramroads were built with a total of 18 inclined planes. There was a great demand for limestone for copper smelting in Swansea and iron making in the valleys, particularly after the process of using local anthracite in iron making was discovered by David Thomas in 1820.

The rottenstone or tripoli was of a very pure quality and was quarried and transported by tram to the Swansea Canal. It was then shipped to London, Germany and the USA to be used in the burnishing of metals. Richard Davies of Ty-coch, a smallholding in Pen-y-Cae, also played an important role in developing the rottenstone business. He was brought up in a non-conformist family and attended Nant-y-Ffin Chapel. He saved most of his wages from working at Glynllech Farm and eventually purchased a lease on part of the Wern Mountain. He made a large profit when the railway was constructed in later years and was able to buy a substantial piece of the Cribarth mountain with its rich mineral deposits. He also constructed a tramline across the Cribarth to transport the rottenstone to the head of the Swansea Canal.

In 1862 an act of Parliament created the Dulais Valley Mineral Railway, built by Isambard Kingdom Brunel, to transport goods to the docks at Briton Ferry. The line was soon incorporated into the Neath and Brecon Railway, extending the route to Brecon via Coelbren and Penwyllt. There was also a regular passenger service from Neath to Brecon. Adelina Patti part funded the passenger station at Penwyllt, also known as Craig-y-Nos Station, after improving the road from Craig-y-Nos to Penwyllt.

William Watkins inherited the whole of William Shaxby's estate and became a very wealthy man. On retiring he built Ty-mawr Mansion in Abercrave and spent most of his retirement greatly involved with the local chapels, Tyn-y-coed and Nantyffin, and later founded Bethlehem, drawing up the plans and offering financial help. He died in 1863 and is buried at Tyn-y-coed. The William Watkins family tomb is near the

Hibbert Archives

William Watkins family tomb, Tyn-y-coed Chapel - 2010

Morgan Morgan family tomb, Callwen - 2010

Hibbert Archives

entrance to Tyn-y-coed Chapel, Abercrave, and consists of three box tombs. My great great grandfather, William (Billy) Morgan, and his wife Ann, William Watkins' daughter, are buried in the tomb - described in William's memorial as a 'box tomb with a splendid slate top'.

William Watkins and his wife Rachel (Shaxby) had six children. On his death Mary, Margaret and Rachel were alive, but Ann, William and Thomas had died prior to 1863. William Watkins's daughters, Mary and Ann were to marry two brothers, Morgan and William (Billy) Morgan respectively, sons of David 'Garth' Morgan of Abercrave.

William Watkins' eldest daughter, Mary, appears to have been the major beneficiary in his will, which included mining interests, and property such as Nant-y-Gwared Farm, Craig-y-Nos. His other daughter Ann had died in 1855 and her widower, William (Billy) Morgan, inherited Glantwyni Farm - later known as Blaentwyni. Morgan Morgan had now become very wealthy, and was able to further develop his mining and farming and property interests in Abercrave and Craig-y-Nos. In April 1856 he was appointed the High Constable for the Division of Ystradgynlais for the ensuing year.

After their marriage, Morgan Morgan lived with Mary at Maes-y-fron Farm, where he also quarried limestone. He had leased a stone quarry to the Blackburn family, high up on the Drum Mountain above Abercrave, where a rich seam of anthracite was found. In the late nineteenth century Morgan formed the Abercrave Collieries Company to run Abercrave and Gwaunclawdd Collieries. Her Majesty's Inspector of Mines survey around 1900 showed William Morgan, Morgan Morgan's son, as the mine manager of Abercrave colliery.

The 1871 census showed Morgan Morgan living in Hen Noyadd, a farm he extensively renovated, and his son William living in Ty-mawr, the country house built by William Watkins. It seems that William was more involved with the mining company whilst his father Morgan Morgan's main interest, as he approached retirement, was farming. In 1875 he acquired Craig-y-Nos Castle, before selling it on to Adelina Patti.

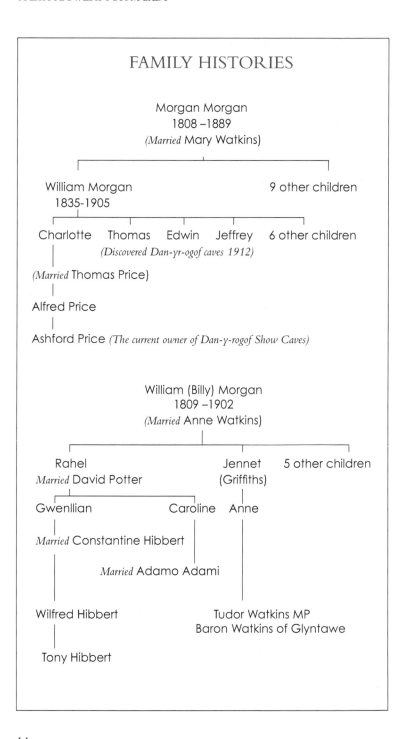

FAMILY HISTORIES

Morgan Morgan
1808 –1889
(Married Mary Watkins)

William Morgan
1835-1905

9 other children

Charlotte Thomas Edwin Jeffrey 6 other children
(Discovered Dan-yr-ogof caves 1912)

(Married Thomas Price)

Alfred Price

Ashford Price *(The current owner of Dan-y-rogof Show Caves)*

William (Billy) Morgan
1809 –1902
(Married Anne Watkins)

Rahel
Married David Potter

Jennet 5 other children
(Griffiths)

Gwenllian Caroline Anne

Married Constantine Hibbert

Married Adamo Adami

Wilfred Hibbert

Tudor Watkins MP
Baron Watkins of Glyntawe

Tony Hibbert

William inherited the coal mines and developed them to a high standard. It was William's sons, Jeff, Tommy and Edwin, who squeezed through a tiny passage at the mouth of the Llynfell river in 1912 and discovered Dan-yr-ogof Caves, but that is a later story.

The Morgan family owned and built houses in the area, many to provide homes for the families of mineworkers. I was born in Pen-y-bont cottages, owned by the Morgans, opposite Dan-yr-ogof caves. They have now been demolished and replaced by one dwelling. I later moved to Craig-y-Nos Bungalow. At the time of the 1881 census Morgan Morgan owned Nant-y-Gwared Farm, Craig-y-Nos, but retired to the Pentre Cribarth Farm, Craig-y-Nos, and died there in 1889. He chose to be buried at Callwen Church and not Tyn-y-coed, his wife's family tomb.

William (Billy) Morgan lived at the Dderi Farm, Glyntawe, after his marriage to Anne Watkins in 1837, before moving to Glantwyni Farm. Billy Morgan seems to have been content to continue with his farming in Glyntawe after the premature death of his wife Ann in 1855. At the time of the 1871 census he was still farming at Glantwyni, but by the 1891 census he had retired to live with his daughter Elizabeth and son-in-law, William Powell Watkins, at Ongur Uchaf Farm. William Powell Watkins was a tenant of Ongur Uchaf, which by 1888 was owned by Adelina Patti.

Constantine Hibbert, Patti's head gardener, and his wife Gwen started their married life in 1891, living with Gwen's grandfather Billy and her aunt Elizabeth in a flat at Ongur Uchaf. They lived there for a few years before taking up residence at the gardener's cottage in the grounds of Craig-y-Nos Castle. It seems Patti had converted Ongur Uchaf into flats. The 1891 census shows that there were eight people in addition to the Watkins family residing at Ongur Uchaf. Four of these were decorators from London, presumably working on Patti's theatre prior to the grand opening in 1891. They were probably employed by George Jackson & Sons, creators of fine interior plasterwork. The same firm worked on Drury Lane Theatre, which was claimed to be part of the inspiration to build the Patti Theatre). Carl Grafe, 'Artiste Music', and Thomas Henry Davies, a young assistant butler, also lived in the flats.

Billy Morgan died at Ongur Uchaf in 1902 at the age of ninety-two. He was buried with his wife Ann in the William Watkins family tomb at Tyn-Y-Coed Chapel, Abercrave. It was Billy Morgan's daughter Rahel who was to marry David Potter, from Sussex. This was the first generation of Swansea Valley 'Potters' - a name which is common in the area today.

Two

THE GROWTH OF A COMMUNITY

The Glyntawe – Craig-y-Nos – Penwyllt triangle was to witness great changes in the second half of the nineteenth century. Glyntawe and Craig-y-Nos consisted mainly of hill farmers whilst the 1841 census recorded two households living in Penwyllt. All this was to change over the next forty years, particularly in Craig-y-Nos and Penwyllt. The building of Craig-y-Nos in about 1843, and its subsequent sale to Adelina Patti in 1878, provided a new sector of employment in the area and attracted employees from other parts of the UK and abroad. Mining activity on the Cribarth mountain was at its peak, which offered alternative employment to working the land.

Many people migrated to Penwyllt to satisfy the needs of the limestone and silica brick industries. Penwyllt's population increased from about three families in 1871 to several hundred inhabitants by 1891.

Theophilus Jones in his History of the County of Brecknock explains that in around 1842 Rice Davies Powell, the son of a local doctor William Powell, (who also claimed to be a descendant of Brychan Brycheiniog), purchased a field known as Cae Bryn Melin Bach, across the road from Pentre Cribarth farm, in Craig-y-Nos. Rice Davies Powell had inherited a great deal of money from his mother's father, the wealthy merchant, Rice Davies. He commissioned the local architect T.H. Wyatt to design and construct the mansion we know today as Craig-y-Nos Castle. Wyatt also designed the Shire Hall in Brecon, now the museum, Malpas Court and Llandogo Priory. The original mansion was built as a 'castle like structure', probably using stone from the local limestone quarries. Its magnificent location faced the Craig-y-Rhiwarth mountain, adjacent to Penwyllt on one side and the Cribarth mountain on

The original Craig-y-Nos Mansion
(above and below) built by Rice Davies Powell

the other. Rice Davies Powell overspent on the project and it was left unfinished, although he lived there at the time when he was High Sheriff of Brecknockshire.

His time at Craig-y-Nos was surrounded by tragedy. His wife died at the age of thirty-seven and four of his six children died at an early age. Rice Davies Powell himself died at fifty-seven, in 1862. Craig-y-Nos was inherited by his two daughters, Harriet and Gwladys. Gwladys married and went to live in South America and Harriet took up residence in Craig-y-Nos with her husband, Captain William Augustus Hamilton Kinnaird Allaway. He is listed as a Brecknockshire Magistrate in 1871, living in Craig-y-Nos.

Tragedy again struck and Captain Allaway died at the age of twenty-nine in 1874. The 1871 census shows Samuel Williams and his wife Ann living in Craig-y-Nos, but no Captain Allaway or his wife Harriet: they were probably away at the time of the census. By 1891 Samuel Williams and his wife had moved to 3 Pen-y-bont Cottages near Dan-yr-ogof Caves, and Samuel's occupation was listed as general labourer. Samuel and his wife were probably employed by Allaway at the castle, and lived there at the time of the 1871 census. When Captain Allaway died, the castle was purchased from the Chancery Court in 1875 by Morgan Morgan, son-in-law of William Watkins, a local farmer and industrialist.

The Morgan family lived at the castle for only a short time before selling the property to Adelina Patti in 1878. Morgan Morgan moved to Pentre Cribarth Farm across the road from the castle. It is highly likely this property came with the castle purchase from the Rice Davies Powell family. Adelina Patti bought the castle, with about 17 acres, for £3,500. Morgan Morgan retained a large area of the land in close proximity to his new farm, presumably to increase the size of Pentre Cribarth.

Good examples of the influx of labour into the area in the mid to late 1800s were my grandfather, who came to Craig-y-Nos from Derbyshire in 1889, and my great grandfather, David Potter, who arrived in the upper Swansea Valley from Sussex in 1848 to work at the remote Cefn Cul Farm, Glyntawe, as a warrener.

Cefncul Farm Glyntawe 2004

John Potter's Headstone, Callwen Church. Died 1880 aged 22 years

David Potter was from Worthing in Sussex, and was employed by Sir Curtis Miranda Lampson. He was twenty-two when he moved into Cefn Cul with agent John Thomas Blazey, from Norfolk, and a house servant, Susan Farrow, the daughter of Jonathan Farrow, a warrener from Suffolk who lived with his family at Cwm-Crai at the time of the 1851 census. Jonathan Farrow also probably worked for Sir Curtis Miranda Lampson.

Sir Curtis Lampson (1st Baronet) was an Anglo American fur merchant, best remembered for his promotion of the transatlantic telegraph cable. He moved to London in 1830 and established the business of C M Lamson & Company and became a naturalised British Citizen in 1849. He was Director of the Atlantic Telegraph Company and Deputy Governor of the Hudson's Bay Company. David Potter and Thomas John Blazey worked warrens built by Hopkin Morgan and Llewellyn Jones and produced thousands of rabbits annually, primarily for the fur trade. John Blazey soon returned to London but corresponded frequently with David Potter.

On arriving at Cefn Cul my great grandfather, David Potter, did not enjoy the best of health. Cefn Cul was in the bleakest of areas, 1125ft above sea level and very exposed. The Rev J Jones-Davies, during his time as Curator of Brecon Museum, recorded in the Museum News details of David Potter's life and the correspondence he received from his mother and colleagues at that time. Twelve letters were donated to Brecon Museum by Mrs Vi Davies of the Bear House, Trecastle, daughter of Harriet Davies (née Potter), my grandmother's sister.

Anne Potter, David Potter's mother, could not write, so a friend, Edward Brannem, wrote letters for her. Jonathen Farrow also wrote to David Potter in 1862 confirming the death of his daughter Susan. He lived in Newport at the time. John Blazey, who originally lived at Cefncul with David Potter, and continued to work for Sir Curtis Miranda Lampson, wrote to David Potter on a regular basis between 1862 and 1879. In one letter, Blazey enquires about Reece, referring to Rees Howells who at this time kept the Gwyn Arms public

Hibbert Archives

The formidable
Rahel Potter

Rahel Potter and daughters
Jessie, Caroline and Harriet

Pen-y-bont Cottages circa 1900 - since demolished

Hibbert Archives

house, and asks about Ann Samuel, who was landlady of the Tavern y Garreg. He also confirms that Susan Farrow had passed away and mentions Hopkin (Morgan) who helped build the large warren at Cefn Cul. Hopkin lodged at the Dderi Farm with Billy Morgan. These letters give a fascinating insight of life in the mid nineteenth century. Death in families was a common occurrence: John Blazey writes to David Potter in 1862:

I have had many upsets since I left Wales but continue in my own house and attend business as usual. We now count eight alive and have buried two since I saw you so you may guess how idle us London people are.

The major communication difficulties of that time are highlighted in one letter written when John Blazey had visited Ystradgynlais:

I was at Ystradgynlais about the 28th April last - and stopped in Swansea for two days. If I could have got a pony when at the Ynyescedwin Arms I would have rode up to Glyntawe. If you think of coming up to London, the best way will be to go to Merthyr. Start from Taff Vale station by the early train, 3rd class, about 7o'clock to Cardiff for the South Wales to Paddington Station, London. When at Paddington ask for the underground railway to Kings Cross - 3rd Class. When there, ask for Groswell Road and you can walk from there to my house in 20 minutes.

John Blazey regularly sent newspapers to David Potter, and at Christmas time David Potter sent turkeys, ducks, chickens, hares, butter and cream to Blazey - all carefully packed in a hamper and sent from Penwyllt Station. In return Blazey sent a hamper containing dolls, pipes, tobacco pouches, clothing and toys. In many letters Blazey writes about the effect of the war between Russia and Turkey, about the labour strikes in London and the current market conditions for his employer Sir Curtis Miranda Lampson.

London
43 Wynyatt St.
Goswell Road,
Dec 12th 1866

Dear Sir,

I duly received yours and was glad to hear you were well and at the same time sorrow to hear Turner was dead. You did not say a word about Rhyl or Billy or the young ones. I was at Ystradgynlais about the 28th of April last and returned with Spencer from Mr. Richard-Lewis's to Swansea & stopped in Swansea 2 days.

If i could have got a Pony when at Ynescedwin Arms I would have rode up to Glyntawe.

Now with regard to your visit to London & Sussex I would advise you to wait the Season Tickets which come out about May or June. I mean the return Tickets they would give you from Saturday until the following Saturday and that at less than half the price it would cost you at this time of the year. I have an Idea I shall be in Wales myself about May next & you could then return with me. If however you think of coming up - the best way will be to go to Merthyr start from there by the early Train 3rd Class about 7 o'clock to Cardiff take the Bus at Taff Vale Station to the South Wales to Paddington Station London - & when at Paddington ask for the underground railway to Kings Cross - 3rd class - when there ask for Groswell Road you can walk from there to my house in 20 minutes easy. Keep the top of this letter for my Directions. Now this will cost you all together 23/- but it will at this time of the year cost 23/- back, but in the Summer you can get a return Ticket to Swansea. I mean from Swansea to London & from London to Swansea for 12/6 3rd class, at same time you can get a return Ticket to Rowfant for 2/6 which now cost 4/10 by riding 3rd class both ways. If you make up your mind to come write me for certain the Train you will leave Cardiff or Swansea by & I'll meet you at Paddington myself. I would write you more but I am now full of business. Our Rabbits this year do not amount to 2,000 and we do not think much of them now. I have not seen Farrow for a long time but I know he is well and last time I was with him he was looking much better than at Cefn Cul. I cannot give you any news about your brothers or sisters. I think one of them was at east Grinstead last Summer. M. Lampson is made a Baronet. his Title is Sir Curtis Miranda Lampson. They are going to build a New Hall at Rowfant he look as well as ever. I cannot spare you more time. Give my Love to your Wife and her Father & all his little ones that were who I suppose are like your own each day growing larger. To Mr & Mrs Howells and all the old Friends at the Gwyn Arms &

I am truly In Haste,
Yours respectfully,
J. T. Blazey.

P.S.   I have just thought there is another route for less money from Merthyr and that is by way of Pontypool. You can see this in any of the Welch Papers. The Silurian a Brecon Paper gives the time and fares.

Haste   Sir C. M. Lampson have got a £10 prize in the Cattle Show It's a Heifer 2 years and 9 months old. I am just going to look at it. I send you a paper with this

London, 1877
Trade here is very bad and I think likely to be worse. If this war
continues and I think it is very likely to last a long time, it will
be finished by the amalgamation of England with some other
continental powers and with a serious loss of life. We look forward
to a very bad and trying winter for all the working classes. These
strikes tend to injure trade of all kinds.

London 1879
Trade of all kinds has improved in London during this last three
months and I think is still looking better. I do sincerely hope there
will be no more strikes. I see papers from all parts of the globe
and the iron trade have it again in their own hand if the men will
only accept fair wages.

The English inhabitants of Cefn Cul were made very
welcome by their neighbours Billy and Anne Morgan of
the Dderi farm, just over the hill and about 500 yards from
Tavern-y-Garreg public house. They had five daughters, the
eldest, Rahel, being thirteen years of age in 1850. David
Potter took a fancy to Rahel, and on 17th March 1856, when
Rahel was nineteen they married at Callwen Church. David
Potter was twenty-eight. Their first child William was born in
December 1856. The 1861 census confirms they were living at
Callwen, with David Potter working as a quarryman. By the 1871
census his fourteen-year-old son William also worked in Penwyllt
Quarries. By 1880 David and Rahel had 13 children.

Rahel Potter's mother Anne (William Watkin's daughter) died
in 1855 at the early age of thirty-seven, leaving a family of five
children under the age of sixteen. Rahel was eighteen and played
a large part in helping her father, William Morgan, raise the family.
With such a large family of her own, after her marriage to David
Potter, her life must have been extremely hard. She was clearly a
strong woman in all respects.

Tragedy struck the Potter family in 1880. Llewellyn and Hannah
Jeffries of Tavern-y-Garreg were married on December 11th.

To celebrate the marriage it was intended to fire a canon on the 'Tasg' - a path on the edge of Craig-y-Rhiwarth, between Penwyllt and Glyntawe. This was the walking route taken by schoolchildren, quarry workers and others travelling to and from the valley. There was a problem with the canon, which exploded, and killed John Potter at the age of twenty-two. He was Rahel and David's second son, and is buried at Callwen Church.

The 1881 census showed that David and Rahel Potter had moved to No. 1 Penwyllt Cottages, Penwyllt. Their eldest son William Potter lived with his wife, Hannah, and daughter Rachel in No. 6. David Potter had left the rapidly declining rabbit fur trade, which had probably ceased to operate, and took employment as a limeburner at the quarry. Limeburning was a major business, with burnt lime being used extensively by the farming and iron making industries. He also spent some time working as a part time gamekeeper at the castle for Adelina Patti. For a short time they lived at Pen-Y-Foel, Penwyllt, a two-room farmhouse, and a quarter-acre smallholding with 13 acres of mountain grazing.

By the 1891 census, Rahel and David Potter had moved from Penwyllt to No. 2 Pen-y-bont Cottages, opposite Dan-yr-ogof Caves, adjacent to the River Llynfell. (The exit of the River Llynfell from Dan-yr-ogof Caves was the point of entry for the Morgan Brothers who were to discover the caves many years later.) The census, if correct, indicated that only Jessie, an adopted daughter raised by Rachel, and Harriet lived at home. David Potter died soon afterwards. Rahel Potter died at Pen-y-Bont in 1907, at the age of seventy, and was buried in Callwen alongside her husband David Potter.

The 1871 census shows the changing pattern of employment in the area and the influx of workers from outside the parish. Penwyllt Cottages were inhabited by an Irish family originally from Kilkenny. The head of the household, Thomas Maher, worked in the limestone quarries. Their lodger was a stonemason from Tipperary.

The census also records a James Tool (Irish) lodging at Penwyllt Cottages and working as a rail road labourer. Charles Cooney, an Irishman, lodged with the Templeton family of Birch Bank

Cottage (opposite Cefn Cul Farm), whose Scottish head of the household was a shepherd, probably employed at Christie's model farm at Cnewr.

Local young men were beginning to take up careers in the quarrying industry. Howell Powell of Blaencar Farm, who was eighteen, and Thomas Samuel, son of the Tavern-y-Garreg Inn, aged twenty-three, were examples of this at that time.

Penwyllt was now becoming a thriving community with the limestone quarries and silica brick works being the major employers. Adelina Patti purchased Craig-y-Nos Castle in 1878. Craig-y-Nos Station in Penwyllt, and the road leading to it would undergo major reconstruction. A public house, Penwyllt Inn, also known as the Stump, was opened to slake the thirst of the limestone and silica brick workers.

Until the late nineteenth century the local children of Penwyllt, Craig-y-Nos and Glyntawe received their elementary education at Pen-y-cae School, just over a mile from Craig-y-Nos, in the direction of Ystradgynlais. With the growth in population in the area, this school was having difficulties meeting the educational needs of the local children. In 1899, the two-classroom Glyntawe School was opened: its location was ideal. Pupils from Craig-y-Nos and Glyntawe could comfortably walk to the new school, whilst its position at the bottom of the 'Tasg' meant the children of parents living in Penwyllt could walk the mile or so down the Tasg every morning, and return by the same route in the evening. Weather conditions in the winter were usually pretty severe and at times extremely difficult for the pupils from Penwyllt and outlying areas, especially the very young.

Glyntawe School records, kept at Powys Archives, record the following in the school managers' minutes for 1903:

A resolution was put forward to the District Committee as follows: We as managers most earnestly beg to draw your attention to the very bad state of the drinking water supply to the above school which is at present running along the surface about 100 yards passing close to a farmyard and sewerage from the cowsheds etc. is running direct to the stream which causes the water to be unfit for drinking.

Heating Glyntawe School was also a major problem in the severe winter months, which I can vouch for as I was a pupil there from 1947 to 1954. The records of December 1916 showed:

A stove be fixed in the upper class room where the heat has been under 40 degrees on many occasions lately, which is injurious to the health of the children, while in the other room it is very little better.

Glyntawe School was also prone to flooding from the Byfre river. There was a particularly severe flood in 1907, when Cwm Byfre House was damaged. Due to the severe winter weather, and the fact the pupils walked to school, illness and poor attendance was a problem. By the time pupils arrived at school they were often wet to the skin. I remember in my days our headmaster, Ithel Llewellyn, making us very welcome hot cups of chocolate in the winter months.

Glyntawe was never a large school but the achievements of its past pupils were commendable. At its peak in 1915 the school had 69 pupils, but as the post war industrial activity in Penwyllt declined only 22 pupils remained at Glyntawe in 1959. When I left in 1954 there were 26 pupils

Three

HOME SWEET HOME

Madam Adelina Patti was born in Madrid in 1843, and was christened Adela Juana Maria Patti. She was the daughter of Italian prima donna, Caterina Barili, and Sicilian tenor, Salvatore Patti. Although born in Madrid, Adelina was very proud of her Italian nationality. As a child she was taken regularly to see her mother perform in opera and this was to have a profound effect on her future career. In 1847 the family moved to New York.

Adelina was very young when she demonstrated her remarkable talent. At the age of seven she gave a faultless performance of *Casta Diva* from Bellini's *Norma*, standing on the kitchen table. She often sang with her parents at the Astor Place Opera House, a Verdi aria or a Jenny Lind song. Max Maretzec, a conductor associated with the Astor, reported her performance at the time, 'to the delight and astonishment of the singers and other persons present'. Her family were amazed, and soon realized that Adelina was indeed very special. Her first public performance was soon to follow – a charity concert at Triplers Hall in New York at the age of just eight. A tour of Canada, Mexico, the USA and Cuba followed. The Patti family had fallen on hard times, but the child prodigy was soon able to restore their good fortune: her first tour earned her $20,000. She became highly successful in America and made her operatic debut in the title role of *Lucia di Lammermoor* at the New York Academy in 1859.

Accompanied by her father, Salvatore, she arrived in England in April 1861. Her first performance at Covent Garden was soon to follow, one month later. Her Covent Garden debut in *La Sonnambula*, closely followed by appearances as *Violetta*, *Lucia*, *Zerlina* and *Rosina*, firmly established her as the great soprano of the day. Madam Adelina Patti was making a name

Adelina Patti – image presented to Con Hibbert

for herself in Europe and was in great demand to sing at many royal palaces, including an invitation from Queen Victoria to sing at Buckingham Palace.

Adelina was becoming extremely wealthy, and at this time lived in Clapham, London, with Karolyn Baumeister (Karo), who was to become her devoted friend and companion for over 50 years. In May 1866 she played *Lucia* to the *Edgardo* of a very ordinary French tenor, Ernesto Nicolini. The press were not kind to Nicolini's performance, and his contract was soon terminated. An 1898 press cutting of his obituary in the Daily Telegraph mentioned this performance:

> *His reception by the audience of the Royal Italian Opera House and the comments passed upon his initial performance by the Metropolitan Press proving, to a certain extent, unsatisfactory, he did not visit London again until April 1871.*

Their paths would cross again and Nicolini would have a big part to play in both the lives of Adelina Patti and Constantine Hibbert.

Patti was now mixing increasingly in royal circles, and became very friendly with the Emperor and Empress in Paris. The Director of Court Cotillions to the Empress was an insignificant little man, Henri, Marquis De Caux, who had his eyes set firmly on the rich prima donna. The Marquis was 18 years older than Patti but he was keen on Patti's wealth and she in turn dreamed of a royal connection. They were married in the Roman Catholic Church, Clapham Common on July 29th 1868. It was not a successful partnership, but things went reasonably well for the first two years.

When Nicolini returned to England in 1871 he performed at Drury Lane to great acclaim. Wilhelm Kuhe, in his *Musical Recollections,* wrote about Nicolini:

> *He was very handsome, his voice was a real tenor of exceeding beauty and most artistically managed, while his acting was both manly and graceful.*

Adelina Patti - print published by Illustrated London News

His ability had vastly improved and he was cast to play alongside Patti in *Romeo and Juliet*. Their styles may have complemented each other but initially Patti had a dislike for Nicolini, who had rented a property next door to Patti and was constantly arguing with his wife – mainly due to his philandering! In 1876 Patti played *Aida* to Nicolini's *Ramades*. The performance was passionate, and Patti must have fallen for Nicolini's charm. She formally separated from the Marquis in 1877 and moved in with Nicolini. They gave memorable performances together, particularly in Italy. Verdi wrote at the time:

She is an artist by nature, so perfect that perhaps there has never been her equal.

It was at this time that Patti declared an interest in Craig-y-Nos Castle. She had travelled extensively from an early age and she longed for a retreat in the country which she could call her home. She would escape the stress and hectic pace of the London circuit. She was now thirty-five years of age. At the age of forty-four Nicolini was keen to live the life of the country squire and pursue his favourite pastimes of hunting and shooting.

Herman Klein, the biographer of Adelina Patti, wrote that Patti and Nicolini stayed for a short while with the Member of Parliament, Sir Hussey Vivian, and his brother, Graham Vivian, at their Swansea home. The Vivians informed Patti and Nicolini that Craig-y-Nos was up for sale and suggested they visit at their earliest convenience. Both Patti and Nicolini were immediately struck by the beauty and scenic location of the mansion: by the end of the visit they were determined to buy the property at any cost. It took them three years to complete the purchase from Morgan Morgan, and in October 1878 they became the proud owners of Craig-y-Nos Castle, together with around 17 acres, for £3500. Mor,gan had paid £8,000 for the castle in 1875 but he retained a great deal of surrounding land, which presumably became part of the Pentre Cribarth Farm, the new Morgan residence. Morgan's main interest was land ownership

To Costantine Hibbert
From   E. Nicolini
Craig-y-nos 21-4-96

Ernesto Nicolini

and farming, having inherited a great deal of assets from his father-in-law, William Watkins. Patti purchased additional land at a later date for future development.

Patti and Nicolni intended to entertain their many friends at Craig-y-Nos, but the original house was too small and extensions would be a priority. The grand plan for the castle was hatched.

Patti had lived with Nicolini, a married man, since buying Craig-y-Nos Castle in 1878, and had attracted criticism from moralists. The California Journal, *The Wasp*, claimed in March 1885 that people went to see her perform, not to hear a great artist, but to see a great wanton − a beautiful sensualist, the fame of whose adulteries had overspread the globe. On Thursday, 10th June 1886 Adelina Patti married Nicolini. The rector of Ystradgynlais Church, Rev E L Davies-Glanley, reported the marriage in London's Pall Mall Gazette:

I believe Madam Patti wishes her marriage to be as public as possible, for probably she is under the impression that the world condemns her life as it is as present.

They were married by the French Consul in Swansea, followed by a religious ceremony in Ystradgynlais Parish Church. Six landaus followed by two 'four in hands' proceeded from Craig-y-Nos Castle to St Cynogs Church in Ystradgynlais, through the decorated streets of Penycae, Abercrave and Caerbont. The locals loved Patti, and on her wedding day she provided refreshments for hundreds of children who lined the route. There were seven hundred guests at the church and the wedding reception held at Craig-y-Nos was a feast. William Beatty-Kingston a reporter for the The Theatre, wrote:

There was a banquet in the Great Hall where the yeomen, trades folk and servants ate their way through several tons of fresh meat, wagon loads of bread and pastries, casks of strong beer.

Patti and her guests celebrated in the Winter Garden at the castle. Letters of congratulations were read out from the Prince

Waterton Hall, near Bridgend, where Patti and
Nicolini lived before moving to Craig-y-Nos

Early photograph of Chatsworth House

of Wales, the Queen of Belgium, the Rothschilds, the Duchess of Newcastle, the Queen of Romania, Lily Langtree, and many other famous admirers.

Madam Patti had big ideas about developing Craig-y-Nos, extending the buildings to include a theatre, and landscaping the gardens. The project was a challenge and she needed a young enthusiastic gardener to execute her ambitious plans. In 1889 she appointed Constantine Hibbert to the position of foreman gardener.

Con Hibbert was born in Upper End, Baslow with Bubnell in the Peak District, on 8th October 1864, the youngest child of Mary and James Hibbert. He had three brothers, George, Thomas and James, and a sister Elizabeth. It was a humble beginning for Constantine, or Con, as he was to be known for the rest of his life. He was destined to follow many of his family into a life of service for the Duke of Devonshire at Chatsworth House, as soon as his elementary education had been completed. Little did he know that the experience he would gain in his formative years at Chatsworth would take him on a journey from the rolling hills of the Peak District of Derbyshire to the Brecon Beacons.

At the age of eleven Con started work at a local farm and spent most of his time tending the potato crops. Two years later he seized the opportunity to start a career at Chatsworth as an apprentice gardener. He loved the outdoor life, and was determined to take full advantage of this excellent opportunity. Chatsworth gave him the best training available at that time. It had employed the very best designers and gardeners over the years, the most famous being Paxton, and he became highly proficient and skilful in every aspect of estate management in the beautiful gardens of Chatsworth House. He left Chatsworth in his early twenties and became foreman gardener with the firm of Dixons in Chester, and later held a similar post at Black Rock near Dublin.

His skills did not go unnoticed, and at the age of around twenty-five was invited to apply for the position of foreman gardener at Craig-y-Nos Castle in Brecknockshire. Patti performed a great deal at the stately homes of the rich and

Craig-y-Nos mid-way redevelopment - no theatre, but
new construction on the left including clocktower

Craig-y-Nos Station, early 1900s

famous. Although there is no evidence available, the bursar at Chatsworth informed me recently it was quite common in those days for the gentry to make recommendations to their circle of friends on possible candidates to fill senior positions. Another common link between the Duke of Devonshire and Adelina Patti would undoubtedly have been William Barron, who was commissioned to design the layout of the gardens at Craig-y-Nos. He had been a pupil of Paxton's at Chatsworth and had lived at Singleton Park in Swansea for many years, so probably contributed to that park's design. He also designed Aberdare Park.

Con was summoned to attend for interview at Craig-y-Nos in 1889. The journey there was long and tedious but he eventually arrived at Penwyllt (Craig-y-Nos) station. This small station was set high on the mountain above Craig-y-Nos, and had taken a new lease of life since Patti had arrived at the castle. In order that she was able to visit London and Covent Garden with little effort, and in great comfort, she had purchased her own railway carriage which was kept at Penwyllt. She had also built a magnificent private waiting room. On arrival at Penwyllt, Con was met by horse and carriage and taken to meet Patti at the Castle.

He was quick to accept the offer of foreman gardener, with accommodation provided at the Ongur Uchaf Farm. His life was to change beyond recognition: he would lead a large workforce and have huge responsibilities for one so young. He enjoyed working for Patti, and it was the start of a close working relationship, which lasted until her death in 1919.

Con's early years were extremely busy as the grand plan at the castle unfolded. Within a year he had been promoted to head gardener, at the age of just twenty-six. He was soon to meet the love of his life, Gwenllian Potter, a local girl, who was also in service as a maid at Craig-y-Nos.

Four

GRAND OPENING OF THE CASTLE

Patti and Nicolini took two years to plan and organise a redevelopment programme for the castle and its surrounding land. The castle, which was originally built of grey limestone, was extensively enlarged with a red sandstone section, which roughly doubled its size. Large quantities of building materials were needed for this project and these were transported to Penwyllt station, and on to Craig-y-Nos by horse and cart. The road to Penwyllt was treacherous, especially the last section from Ongur Uchaf farm to the station. Patti arranged for the road from Bell Fach to Ongur Uchaf to be widened and a new section built from Ongur Uchaf to the station over gentler slopes. This road still serves Penwyllt today, and was used for transporting limestone until the recent closure of the quarry. Constructing the new road also made Patti's journeys to the station much safer before she boarded her train on the Neath to Brecon line, to travel worldwide. This was particularly relevant in the winter months.

A conservatory, winter garden, aviary, clock tower, large stable block, coach house and laundry were erected. When Con arrived at Craig-y-Nos the alterations were in full swing. The ground floor of the new section provided the main bedrooms, dressing rooms, as well as 5 other bedrooms and a gun room. The second floor contained 6 large bedrooms, a spare bedroom, and dressing rooms. There was also a miniature chapel on this floor, with altar, pew, stained glass windows and electric light provided by a generating plant on site. The original building was extensively refurbished and provided 6 bedrooms for visitors, 2 bathrooms, 8 large bedrooms for servants, and a further 5 small bedrooms for servants. The ground floor of the old building contained an office block and French and English kitchens. A 5,000 cubic foot capacity gasometer, and a one ton capacity ice making plant were installed.

Hibbert Archives

Craig-y-Nos Castle in 1893

View across the lake circa 1890 - stocked with fish
to cater for Nicolini's love of field sports

Kind permission of Brecknock Museum & Art Gallery

The most impressive addition was her private theatre. It could seat 150 people. It had a mechanism to raise the floor to stage level, if required, to create a ballroom. The seats, which were not fixed, were upholstered in blue velvet. The walls were divided into arabesqued panels of pale blue, cream and gold, between similarly-coloured fluted pillars. A continuous frieze along the inside walls carried the names of prominent opera composers with the name of Rossini taking pride of place. The backdrop was most impressive. Designed by Walter Ham, it portrayed Madam Patti as *Semiramide*, driving a Roman chariot. The stage had a negative rake so that Patti, being short, was not overshadowed by taller performers.

Patti had commissioned William Barron (1800-1891) to lay out the garden to the east of the castle. Barron had been a pupil of Paxton at Chatsworth, and head gardener at Elvaston Castle. He had a reputation for transplanting mature trees. The garden was a model of Victorian style; a combination of the formal and wild. The kitchen garden was highly productive but labour intensive. It appears that Patti's first head gardener had problems establishing the kitchen garden on the site due to run-off.

Con's first five years at Craig-y-Nos were hectic. The gardens had been transformed and extended quite considerably. For such a young head gardener he had excelled. Patti and Nicolini were delighted with the results of his endeavour, and it was the beginning of a friendship and loyal relationship which would last the 33 years he was employed by the prima donna. Nicolini had his hunting and fishing, Patti had her stately home, with its lavish mini-theatre to entertain her friends and encourage local artists and performers.

In addition to all the work involved in seeing through the 'grand plan' for the grounds of the castle, Con had a few grand plans of his own. He had met a young housemaid at the castle, Gwen Potter, a local girl who had been working for Patti at Craig-y-Nos for some time, along with her sisters Caroline (Carrie), Harriet and Jessie. Gwen was born in 1872, one of 11 children and the daughter of David Potter and Rahel Morgan.

The Winter Garden – Con Hibbert standing

Con Hibbert, right, with another member of Patti's staff

Con married Gwen in 1891. She was nineteen years old and he was twenty-six. There were great celebrations in the castle and the champagne flowed. Adelina Patti and Ernesto Nicolini were known to be very generous to their staff and Patti was pleased to see Con settle down with his new wife Gwen. Gwen's sister Carrie was later to marry Patti's Italian chef, Adamo Adami. Adamo was a very handsome man, from Stresa, Lake Maggiore, Italy.

Their first child, Beattie, was born in 1892, and in 1894 they had their first son, Harold. Con and Gwen then moved from their rooms at Ongur Uchaf Farm into the head gardener's cottage in the grounds of the castle, which would be their home until Con retired. Their second son, Ernest, was born in 1898. He was named after Madam Patti's husband at the time, Ernesto Nicolini, who died the same year.

The years that followed were tragic ones for Con and Gwen. Diphtheria was rife in young children at this time, and Beattie, Harold and Ernest all succumbed. In December 1899 Harold died, at the age of four years, and Ernest died aged one year and four months, soon after. Con and Gwen were distraught, but in 1900 infant mortality was very common and life had to continue.

Con worked closely with Patti and Nicolini on the development of the grounds. The steep slopes in the front of the castle facing the river Tawe were landscaped into terraced lawns. Turf was transported from Ongur Uchaf Farm by horse and cart. Con supervised 30 to 40 full-time and part-time gardeners. Hundreds of trees were planted, mainly pines, rhododendrons, oaks, and ornamental shrubs. New fruit and vegetable gardens were laid out to the north of the castle. Drainage was improved and manure and river sand added.

Con replaced poor quality fruit trees and introduced a stove house, a melon pit, a tomato house, a coleus house, a carnation house and vineries in a framed yard designed by Barron. Records show that around 1900 there was a 96 feet long vinery, and 2 lines of pits and frames, with bunches of Muscat grapes often reaching three and a half pounds in weight. The head gardener's cottage, which is now a museum, was situated at the end of the kitchen garden, near the first artificial lake. The Winter Garden, now the Patti Pavilion in Swansea, was Con's pride and joy.

Patti's gardeners at work, Con second left

Walled kitchen garden and the head gardener's cottage circa 1890

Hibbert Archives

The Winter Garden was constructed around 1890. It was a large rectangular building, 40 feet high and with 7000 feet of glass. Abutilon, tacsonias, passion flowers, palms and tree ferns grew inside. Orchids, begonias, and fuchsias were displayed on stone walls around the internal paths. It was heated by stoves attached to the outside of the building to the west.

Nicolini enjoyed his fishing, and Con set about building another lake on the other side of the river Tawe. This was much larger than the first lake and included an island of rhododendrons. This lake was dug by hand with an army of men. Two new bridges were erected to access the new lake, one swing-bridge and another white bridge - which was later to be swept away by flood water. Con was extremely proud of the successful outcome of this project.

For fishing, Nicolini designed himself a costume slightly reminiscent of Gounod's Faust restored to youth - complete with a long feather in his hat. He also considered himself no mean shot. Patti would infuriate him by feeding the pheasants being reared, at the end of the kitchen garden: they became so tame that they rarely left the garden. Shooting anywhere near the castle was forbidden, and Nicolini had to wait for the tamed birds to fly over the river onto the mountain slopes.

The new theatre opened with an inaugural performance of Act 1 from *La Traviata*, with Patti as *Violetta*, Act III from *Faust* with Patti as *Marguerita*, and Nicolini as *Faust,* supported by singers from London. Arditi was the conductor. Patti was sensational, both in performance and dress. The New York Times on August 13th 1891 described the event as a musical festival at Craig-y-Nos:

Patti threw open her new theatre to the world. Trains arrived throughout the day. Among the arrivals were Sir and Lady Hussey Vivian, the Marquis of Anglesey, the Count de Lille, Mr and Mrs Baerd, Augustus Spalding, Mr and Mrs Klein, Mr Marcus R Mayer, Mlle. Valda, the distinguished prima donna, Mr and Mrs Arditi, and Mr Lely, the rising young tenor. Patti was dressed in pink satin, trimmed with embroidery and roses and she actually blazed with diamonds. Programmes, hand-painted on yellow satin, were served to

Hibbert Archives

Theatre interior in 1920 - drop curtain from *Semiramide*

Con Hibbert, left, with other staff at Craig-y-Nos

Hibbert Archives

the guests. After the evening's performance was over the diva resumed her role of hostess, mingling with guests and having a smile and a shake of the hand for everyone. The neighbours of the fair songstress, who had now for the first time heard her voice, were overcome with admiration, and Patti seemed to enjoy their expressions of surprise and pleasure even more than the more conventional compliments showered upon her by the distinguished guests from abroad. The festivities will be continued on Saturday. The theatre is lavishly decorated, pale-blue tints pre-dominating with a toning of cream and gold. The names of the great composers are inscribed appropriately on the ceiling. Mr Hulley from Swansea provided the music with his twenty-one-piece orchestra, and there were performances twice a day for a fortnight in the theatre.

Prior to the opening ceremony, she entertained all her guests lavishly in the conservatory. It was rumoured that 450 bottles of champagne were consumed. Henry Irving, who was due to make the opening address, failed to attend: the address was delegated to William Terris, an actor from the Lyceum Theatre. Coffee was taken in the billiard room where they listened to Nicolini's choice of music on the ochestrian, a massive electrically-driven organ equipped to play 80 tunes.

During her time at Craig-y-Nos Patti chose her staff very carefully. One of her loyal domestic servants was Lorenzo Couroneu de Patrocini, or Patro as she was known. She and 'Karo' Baumeister, who managed the household and arranged Patti's gowns and jewels, held special positions at the castle.

Some years after she purchased Craig-y-Nos, Patti was dining at the Sackfield Hotel in Dublin. She was so impressed with the food, particularly the soup, that she asked to see the chef. She suggested that if he ever needed a change he should consider a position at the castle. That chef was Adamo Adami, from Stresa in Italy, and he was well known in various circles in Italy, France and Germany. Formerly chef at the Casino in Nice, he afterwards went to the Sackfield in Dublin. He was a colourful character and later a great friend and brother-in law to

Chef Adamo Adami

Longo, Mabel Woodford
(Patti's secretary) and Adami

Patro, right, with other staff

Adami's widow Carrie with
sons Angelo and Antonio

Hibbert Archives

Con Hibbert. He was to spend nine years as chef to Adelina Patti before purchasing the Neuadd Arms Hotel in Llanwrtyd Wells. His obituary in a local paper read:

Mr Adamo Adami, of the Neuadd Arms Hotel, Llanwrtyd Wells, who, at the early age of 43, has just passed away from the effects of double pneumonia, was a king of chefs. It ran in the blood. His grandfather and father, of the Hotel Alpino, Stresa, Lago Maggiore, were noted chefs. There are a large family of brothers, who are also chefs. The eldest brother has for many years been chef at St Andrews Hotel, Buxton, Derbyshire, another is chef at the National Liberal Club in London.

Adamo married Carrie Potter, my grandmother's sister. Carrie also worked for Adelina Patti. They had three children. Adamo was a keen sportsman and his passion was fishing and shooting, which was a good combination at Craig-y-Nos. The castle and surrounding areas provided good hunting. As a boy I was introduced to fishing by Antonio Adami, Adamo's son. Like his father, he was passionate about fishing and very good at it.

Longo was a great friend of Con Hibbert. He was a butler at the time of Nicolini and Cederström. In Nicolini's days he played an important part in the social life at the castle and was known as 'pop the corks Longo'. Ethel Rosate-Lunn wrote about life under Cederström:

On the rare occasions when Patti was alone she would often invite the staff to dress in any fancy dress available, and assemble in the billiard room. Madame, too, would often dress in fancy dress, then she would turn to Longo, the butler, and say, 'Pop the corks Longo,' and we would all, Madame included, drink a glass of champagne. I must add this never occurred when the Baron (Cederström) was in residence at the castle.

William Heck (Wilh Hech), the agent for Patti's estate, was responsible for heating, lighting, ventilation and sanitation. He was the business manager dealing with all correspondence relating to

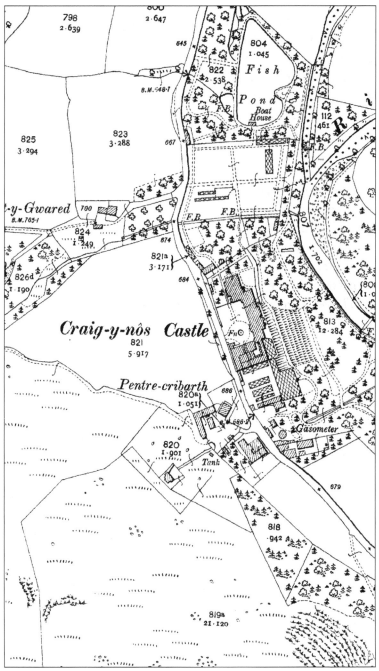

Extract from Ordnance Survey 1:2500 map, 1905

the castle infrastructure, and its grounds. The 1891 census shows him at Craig-y-Nos aged forty years, employed as a steward. After the two lakes were completed it was Heck who supervised the stocking of fish. The local river Tawe was also stocked with trout specially purchased from Scotland.

Ethel Lunn joined Patti's staff at the castle in 1909, towards the end of Patti's life. She describes vividly her arrival at Penwyllt station:

I saw Craig-y-Nos Castle for the first time on a cold, windy day of March 1909. I had travelled from my home in Staffordshire, arriving at Penwyllt, the station for Craig-y-Nos. Fred Rivers, the coachman from the castle, met me. He picked up my luggage and carried it outside to the waiting trap. I followed and looked around at the endless mountains, bare and bleak for winter. My spirits, already low, sank still further. 'Where in heaven's name have I come to?' I asked in dismay. The coachman smiled and said, 'You wait a while – you will love it,' he assured me. 'Oh no I won't,' I exclaimed bitterly. 'A month from now you will be bringing me back to the station.' (She stayed in Patti's employ for five years.)

Ethel was Patti's head laundry maid and in later years she would often recall Patti's dislike of the stiffness of starched clothing. On one occasion, in a fit of temper, she caught hold of a garment and ripped it to shreds. Of course, with it being so rigid, it was quite easy to tear.

She was a close friend of Gwen and Con Hibbert and Gwen and Dai Price, the gamekeeper. Dai's father had been head gamekeeper in the time of both Nicolini and Cederström. Dai Price later became landlord of the Gwyn Arms public house in Glyntawe. In later life Ethel Lunn often stayed with Con and Gwen at their retirement home, Craig-y-Nos Bungalow. She was well known in Craig-y-Nos for her poetry, most of it dedicated to her close friends in the upper Swansea Valley, and for her vivid descriptions of the natural beauty of the area.

Five

THE CURTAIN STARTS TO FALL

Patti intended that the new theatre would be fully utilised, and she encouraged amateur artists from South Wales to perform at the castle so that she could assess their ability. Con's daughter, Violet, would later benefit from this gesture. The first such performance took place soon after the official opening, a pantomime entitled *Life at Hamilton Castle*. This was followed by *Forsaken*. Patti took the lead parts in both events, with occasional performances by Nicolini.

In 1892 and 1893 Patti toured America, and her audiences were captivated by the old favourites: *The Last Rose of Summer, Coming Through The Rye*, and *Home Sweet Home*. At the end of the season she performed at the New York Metropolitan Opera House in *Lucia* and *Il Barbiere di Siviglia*: this was the last time she appeared on the American opera stage.

When she returned home her energy was again directed towards performances in Craig-y-Nos theatre. She presented *Kathleen Mavoureen* as a ballet d'action, and *Black Eyed Susan*, with Patti taking the part of *Susan*. In December 1894 a matinee called *Love Levels All* was presented as a ballet in three acts. The theatre was not only a platform for entertaining local dignitaries and friends, but she used it to explore the medium of mime, in which she was to become very skilled. Adelina Patti was commanded to sing privately before Queen Victoria in 1894, at Windsor Castle, and was presented with a fine brooch-pin fashioned with the royal crown and monogram.

During her time at Craig-y-Nos, Patti was visited by royalty – Prince Henry of Battenburg and the Crown Prince of Sweden. Many authors have written that Patti was visited at Craig-y-Nos by the Prince of Wales, but I was told on many occasions by my grandfather Con that he never actually made it. He arrived in

Baron Cederström

Swansea but his car was too wide for the Swansea Valley roads. Instead he 'took tea' with Miss Talbot at Penrice Castle.

Patti's last performances in a full production at Covent Garden were in 1895, when she was invited to sing at the recently restored opera house. Her first performance was in *La Traviata* in June that year. Act III was stunning. Patti wore a white dress on which were mounted all her diamonds, worth an estimated £200,000, and previously removed from their settings. She appeared six times at Covent Garden that season and this ended her commercial career on the opera stage.

In 1895 she invited the elite of Brecknockshire and Glamorganshire to attend a special matinee at Craig-y-Nos. It was called *Mirka L'enchantresse*, and was dedicated to Patti. This was of such importance to her that she engaged the services of Frank Rego, from the Abbey and Grau theatres in the USA, and late of Covent Garden, to manage the scenic effects. Florence Crews, who had won the National Eisteddfod pianoforte competition the previous week, was introduced to the audience and Patti congratulated her on her success. Patti herself had sung *Land of My Fathers* and *Home Sweet Home* at the National Eisteddfod in Brecon in 1889.

Patti went on to present many more events at Craig-y-Nos, demonstrating that her original objectives for the theatre had been achieved. She had transformed a country mansion in beautiful surroundings into a magnificent castle, alive with vibrant music. She was indeed the Queen of Song and the Queen of Craig-y-Nos.

Over the years she had made a huge contribution to various local charity events. Local press called her Lady Bountiful of Cwmtawe. Her first charity concert was in Swansea in 1882, which raised £830 for Swansea Hospital. In semi-retirement her concerts continued in each of the three main towns of Brecon, Swansea and Neath, in turn, and sums varying between £700 and £800 were raised for the benefit of Swansea Hospital, Brecon Infirmary, the Rest Home at Porthcawl, and the Patti Funds for the poor of Brecon and Neath. She was treated like royalty

Ethel Rosate Lunn – Patti's Head Laundry maid

More of Patti's staff circa 1900

Hibbert Archives

Hibbert Archives

as she stepped down from her private coach in these towns, but her favourite town was undoubtedly Brecon. She was made an honorary Burgess of the Ancient Borough of Brecon in 1897. Unfortunately, Nicolini was too gravely ill to accompany her. Patti was still very wealthy and continued to command high fees for her performances. Throughout the 1890s, Nicolini's health was deteriorating rapidly and he was suffering from liver and kidney failure. He died in Pau, France, on January 18th, 1898, at the age of sixty-four. Nicolini was a very pleasant and generous man and was sorely missed by the locals and staff of Craig-y-Nos. Con Hibbert would remark in future years that life at Craig-y-Nos with Nicolini at the helm was tremendous fun, and champagne flowed like water. Patti and Nicolini had enjoyed performing together at the castle, playing all the principal parts. They had been a loving couple both on and off the stage. All the joy and celebration was now over.

Six months later a new face would appear at the castle, Adelina's new love, Baron Cederström. Swedish born, Cederström was a director of his own health gymnastic institute in London, and son of Baron Claes Erdad Cederström. It was rumoured that he visited Craig-y-Nos in the years prior to Nicolini's death, in his capacity as an instructor to a health gymnasium. Patti had yearned all her life for a title and this was her chance.

On the 25th January, 1899, Patti married Baron Olaf Cederström in the Roman Catholic church in Brecon, and she became Baroness Cederström. She was fifty-six and he was twenty-eight. They both became British subjects.

The New York Times on the 26th January, 1899 carried a full account of the celebrity wedding. It was was a fine affair, with Patti taking her train from Craig-y-Nos to Brecon, and being met at Brecon station by the band of the South Wales Borderers. The wedding party travelled to the church in five specially decorated landaus.

Patti was radiant in an embroidered dress of dove-coloured satin with a bodice of pale grey and a bonnet trimmed with mauve orchids. The aldermen of Brecon, in their robes of office, met the bride and bridegroom in the porch of the church. The

Pullman Carriage 'Craig-y-Nos' used by Patti on her
American / Canadian tour 1903-04

Adelina Patti and her entourage on pullman car Craig-y-Nos

procession to the church, and back to the station, passed under several triumphal arches bearing inscriptions in honour of the bride. Crowds of well-wishers lined the streets to catch a glimpse of their favourite diva.

The wedding breakfast was in Patti's train as it sped to London. Patti's chef had prepared a most elaborate meal on a 30 feet-long table. The dinner service, silver and wines were all supplied from Craig-y-Nos. Patti and Cederström stayed overnight at the Hotel Cecil in London, before spending their honeymoon in the South of France.

Whereas Nicolini was very generous to the staff at Craig-y-Nos, Cederström was less so. My grandfather often commented about this. He felt Cederström was concerned about Patti's future income as she was now in semi-retirement. Cederström set about tightening the budget. He also disliked partying and entertaining, and the mood in the castle was somewhat sombre after many years of 'living it up' with Nicolini.

The theatre was now little used and in 1901 Patti went so far as to place Craig-y-Nos on the market for sale, probably at the suggestion of Cederström. It attracted very little interest, and was soon withdrawn from sale. Patti was highly delighted to continue with her life at the castle. She loved the area and was now part of the community. She was to live there for another 18 years.

On 22nd February, 1900, Patti made her last public operatic performance, at Covent Garden. It was 39 years after she had made her debut at this theatre. She did continue to give concerts, mainly at the Albert Hall and in autumn tours of the provinces. She continued her concerts for charity, in Stockholm and in Brecon in 1900, in Paris in 1901 and in Brecon again in 1902 when she sang for the borough's poor and needy.

In 1903 she made her authorized final tour to the USA. Previous tours had been labelled final, but without her consent. The tour was planned for 60 concerts and, despite some poor reviews from critics, it is recorded that she earned 200,000 dollars for 52 appearances – cancelling the final 8 concerts due

Christmas card to Constantine from Patti's butler
Longo Giacomo - a good friend of Con's

Two record labels from recordings
originally made at Craig-y-Nos

to fatigue. She was, after all, nearly sixty-one years of age. She travelled the USA in a 72 feet-long rail pullman car named 'Craig-y-Nos'.

The late 1890s saw the beginning of sound recording and the development of the Gramophone Company, later known as His Master's Voice. It was in HMV's commercial interest to ensure they recorded all the top names in the music industry, and early recordings of Caruso helped to raise the status of the company. Caruso was virtually unknown in Britain until the sale of his records. By the end of 1905 the company had a very impressive catalogue of names, including Melba, the 'Queen of Covent Garden', De Lucia, Tamango, Joachim, Plancon and Greig. One very important name was missing - Adelina Patti. By 1905 she was something of a national institution, one which Fred Gaisberg, HMV's chief recordist, could ill afford to ignore. He was later to write:

I have always instinctively felt that Patti was the only real diva I have ever met – the only singer who had no flaws for which to apologise.

Patti herself was fairly uninterested in the possibility of recording her voice and had not been very impressed with recordings made of other artists. She treated it as a novelty. Gaisberg clearly had his work cut out in persuading her to agree to the concept. The year she finally consented to make a record was the year she celebrated the fiftieth anniversary of her debut. HMV also faced competition from other record companies. Patti eventually agreed but with certain conditions. The recording had to be made in Craig-y-Nos, as Gaisberg put it, 'a draughty mansion in a somewhat inaccessible part of Wales', and no records were to be released without the test pressings being approved by Patti. She also insisted that the labels on the records would be coloured pink, a colour not to be used by any other artist.

There was a great deal of excitement at Craig-y-Nos leading up to Christmas 1905. Fred Gaisberg and his brother Will arrived with their cumbersome and primitive recording equipment: the microphone had not been invented. A bus brought them from Craig-y-Nos station, now Penwyllt, to the castle where they were greeted by Mr Alcock, Patti's agent at the time. A huge amount of machinery was set up in two large bedrooms Patti had set aside for the recording. Patti was overawed by it all and particularly concerned by the long funnel into which she would direct her voice. It was an ordeal for her to stand still, totally against her Italian temperament, where expressing herself in sudden body movements was only natural.

The system was very primitive and Gainsberg was at times during the recording forced to physically move Patti away from the horn if a high note was imminent. Patti was extremely temperamental and moody and one minute poured compliments on her guests then later would be rude. It took Gaisberg two days to persuade Patti to commence recording. To reward Gaisberg and his brother for the prolonged wait, she instructed her staff to supply them with champagne for their dinner.

The recording, with Landon Ronald accompanying, yielded 14 records of songs and arias. It was launched in February 1906 with advertisements in 200 British newspapers, and record stores displayed long streamers in their windows spelling out the news that Patti had cut a record. Her record was sold at a special price of twenty-one shillings.

Patti was so pleased with the outcome that she made further recordings in June 1906. She was aware of the technical limitations of recording in those days, and of course, she was sixty-two years of age: her voice was not in its prime!

Gaisberg returned to London extremely pleased with his work at Craig-y-Nos. Con was instructed by Patti to ensure Gaisberg travelled back to London with bunches of flowers from the Winter Garden, and braces of pheasants from the butler.

In December 1906 Patti travelled to London to give her final professional concert at the Albert Hall. Prior to the concert she had been interviewed by *The Graphic*, describing her decision to retire as irrevocable:

Am I sorry? Of course I am. My friends are so kind and I love singing, but I am getting tired of it all. I shall sing for the poor. There is much that one ought to do for the poor, and though I have always done what I can, I want to do more.

After her concert *The Daily Telegraph* described her London farewell:

Will any deny her right to be described as historic? To praise her singing is almost an impertinence: the rarest beauty of phrasing; the perfection of the technical command, and the grace and elegance of the style. Will any forget that literally marvellous trill?

In 1907 the diva gave 17 concerts on her farewell provincial tour which included Paris. One of her most memorable charity concerts was the opening of the Pontardawe Institute and Hall, on May 6th, 1909. The locals gave her a tremendous welcome and the local press, *The Cambrian Daily Leader*, reported:

Almost every house flew its flag, and streamers were hung at frequent intervals. Near the institute there was an arch of welcome, built in imitation of a castellated Roman gateway. Over it a Welsh harp glittered in the bright sunshine.

In October that year, while at Newcastle-on-Tyne, she had sad news that Patro, her faithful personal maid, had passed away at Craig-y-Nos. Patro was buried in Callwen Church, Glyntawe.

Six

TWENTIETH CENTURY CRAIG-Y-NOS

The gardener's cottage in the grounds of the castle had now become home to Con Hibbert and his family. The family increased in size with three sons; Wilfred, my father, Alexis and Hector, and a daughter Violet who was born at the cottage. Violet was named after Patti's favourite flower.

Patti was very generous, and Con and his family lived well. He received an allocation of fresh vegetables and fruit from the kitchen gardens and hothouses. Peaches, grapes and nectarines were grown in abundance. Hunting and fishing continued at the castle, when in season, and there was no shortage of trout and game on the Hibbert's dining table. The hunting also provided additional employment for the quarrymen of Penwyllt, who spent days at the castle working as grouse beaters. Gwen's father, David Potter, had been a gamekeeper at the castle before he died, but had also worked in the Penwyllt quarry. He put his background as a warrener to good use when needed at the castle.

Now that Patti had retired and her worldwide travels were curtailed, she was keen to take a greater interest in the locality in which she now lived. She developed a close relationship at this time with Con and his family. Each afternoon she would walk along the main road, past the castle, or through the beautiful gardens, and call on Gwen to see the children. My grandmother told me she was particularly fond of Hector, their eldest surviving son, and would ruffle his beautiful head of hair. She would always sit in the same chair in the cottage, and on one occasion stayed to watch Gwen bath all the children in a tub in front of the fire. She was very excited and immediately called the Baron from the garden to witness the event. Patti never had children.

When Violet was old enough, Patti encouraged her to play the piano and she was eventually to become a very accomplished musician and teacher. At the age of nine Patti invited her to play in one of the concerts at Craig-y-Nos theatre.

Con and Gwen were blissfully happy raising their family in such beautiful and healthy surroundings. Con managed the estate with great efficiency, and the grounds displayed the results of the high standard of workmanship he demanded from himself and his staff. The pines were now maturing and Patti was convinced that regular walks through the pines would help to keep her voice and chest in excellent condition.

Anecdotes about life at Craig-y-Nos handed down through the family were numerous. I was told one such story by Tom Davies of the Gelli Farm, and former stable lad at the castle. He recalled Con mowing the tennis courts with a horse driven grass cutter. During the operation the horse lifted its tail, so Con swiftly removed his bowler hat and caught the flying manure before it hit the ground and damaged the grass surface.

Patti continued with her concern and respect for her staff and the local inhabitants of Craig-y-Nos. She suffered with bouts of rheumatism, a common complaint in the sometimes cold and wet climate of the Breconshire mountains. Con had also been suffering with arthritis in his fingers, and had casually told Patti about his problem. Patti had seen a ring advertised which claimed to alleviate such a complaint and her immediate response was to purchase one and present it to Con. She would often ask Con if the ring worked: he was very diplomatic and would reply, 'Yes, M'Lady'.

Head laundry maid, Ethel Rosate-Lunn, recalls in her book, *My Recollections of Madam Patti*, how she was also ticked off one cold November day for not wearing something around her shoulders as she stepped out into the cold air from the steaming laundry. That evening Patti sent her a shawl which she had to wear, which caused some amusement with her work colleagues.

The Hibbert children were now growing up and Beattie, the eldest, was in her teens. One day Beattie and her friend Gwen

Price, of the Gwyn Arms, were seen untying a boat to row on the lake. They were spotted by Madam Patti and Odile, her personal maid, who were frightened the boat would capsize. Patti called on Gwen and asked her to ensure it did not happen again. Con's family still enjoyed the 'good life', and Patti took it upon herself to see that the whole family were well cared for. One example was the constant supply of chicken received for the Hibbert dining table. Patti ate a lot of chicken, breast only, and the rest would be sent to Gwen.

My grandfather told a story of Patti's concert for charity in 1894, in the Albert Hall, Swansea, which was in aid of Swansea Hospital and the poor of the neighbourhood. There was a large party of dignitaries staying at Craig-y-Nos and they were driven to Swansea in several carriages. Passing through Swansea, one of the gentlemen raised his hat to the crowds and off blew his wig, much to the delight of Adelina Patti.

Patti's contribution to the local economy was enormous. She bought all her meat, eggs and milk locally, but was a stickler for quality and did not hesitate to return any inferior goods if need be on the advice of her chef.

Henry Morgan, of the Gwyn Arms public house, had his own slaughter house and supplied meat to Adelina Patti. His daughter Mrs Price, who owned the Gwyn Arms when I was a boy, helped her father to deliver the meat to the castle. She once related the story of Patti rejecting 15 chicken carcasses because of inferior quality, even though they were only meant to be used for chicken soup! Mrs Price married Dai Price, a gamekeeper at the castle.

Patti's kindness to other people knew no bounds. If she met a tramp or a gypsy on the main road outside the castle, she would always offer them food and send them to the castle kitchens to be fed. It is said she always kept some of the proceeds from her charity concerts to distribute to the needy around Craig-y-Nos. In a letter to her nephew in December 1892, she referred to a Christmas tea she had provided for over 3,000 children, and of the money she gave to the needy:

Hibbert Archives

Card sent to one of Patti's staff, during the Great War: "We hope for 1915 that we will have lasting peace and will never be in conflict again"

Card forwarded to the Carlton Hotel, London - Patti's favourite London hotel where she was probably staying at the time

Hibbert Archives

I gave my annual distribution of money to all the poor old people of the district. It was a most touching sight and everyone, myself included, cried.

Ynyscedwyn school records include some other examples of her kindness. An 1892 entry records a day when she gave a treat of tea and cake to the children, and in the afternoon she and a large number of friends visited the school to see the children partaking of the same. An 1889 entry refers to the closing of the school for half a day to attend Madame Patti's distribution of charities at the village of Ystradgynlais.

Baron Cederström had a huge influence on Patti's lifestyle, and many of her old friends ceased to visit Craig-y-Nos. Houseguests were in the main family members. Patti spent a great deal of time in the company of her new husband's family, making frequent trips to their home in Sweden. By 1909 the number of staff at Craig-y-Nos had fallen to 18.

Ethel Rosate-Lunn recalled the wonderful time they had at Craig-y-Nos at Christmas. Patti would visit the servants' dining hall to sing along with them, drink champagne and wish them a Happy Christmas. There was always a Christmas tree in the theatre, with presents, and in the evening there would be a staff dance when Patti danced with the senior male staff and her husband danced with the head girls. Patti would then sit near the tree and call each person by name to receive his or her gift. The men usually received purses with money and the ladies were given lengths of material for making dresses.

On New Year's Day the local children called for the traditional 'calennig', when they would wish Madam Patti a 'Blwyddyn Newydd Dda', or 'Happy New Year', and were given a sixpenny piece and an apple and orange.

Patti continued to sing in local charity concerts and made appearances at public functions. In 1912 she was enrolled as an honorary freewoman of the Borough of Swansea. She was the only woman in Great Britain at this time to be honoured by two boroughs – Swansea and Brecon.

Con, centre, with members of his team of gardeners

River Llynfell enters Dan-yr-ogof Caves – entry point for Morgan Brothers

At this time there was major activity of a different kind a short distance away from the castle. Three brothers, Jeff, Edwin and Tommy Morgan, were busy exploring the mouth of the River Llynfell with Morgan Williams, a local gamekeeper. Jeff, Edwin and Tommy were the sons of William Morgan, Tymawr, a first cousin of Rahel Potter, my great grandmother. Little did they know that they were about to discover one of the great wonders of Wales, the Dan-yr-ogof Caves.

They had found a dry cave above the river cave and explored it up to a large pool. A coracle was brought and Tommy Morgan rowed 40 yards across the lake, then 20 yards along a tunnel landing near the foot of a cataract. His fellow explorers pulled the coracle back with string, and all four eventually made it across the lake. In total they crossed four lakes. Considering the primitive equipment they had, just candles and oil lamps, this was no mean feat.

By 1937 the Morgan brothers had purchased the land surrounding the cave and invited E Roberts of the Yorkshire Ramblers Club to explore the cavern. He was accompanied by Messrs Platten, Nelstrop and Gowing. There was a large number of people taking part in the exploration at that time, including the Morgan brothers, Ashford Price and David Price, of the Gwyn Arms public house. Platten seemed to be in charge.

A new entrance was blasted in 1939 above the river exit, making it an easy walk into the cavern. A water turbine was installed to generate electricity for the cave lighting and the cave was open to the public for a short time that year. Further exploration in the 1960s by the South Wales Caving Club led to the complex being opened again to the public, becoming one of Britain's major natural attractions.

1914 saw the onset of war. At the age of seventy-one, Adelina Patti made a rare appearance at a London concert to aid the cause. This was the last time she ever sang in public – 24th October, 1914. She visited the wounded in local hospitals, knitted scarves for the frontline soldiers and sailors, and gave money to the local families whose men were at the front.

Hibbert Archives

Hibbert family in early 1920s

rear - Hector, Wilf, Alexis   *front* - Beattie, Con, Gwen, Violet

Confirmation of seed order to Con Hibbert from
Sutton Seeds at the Royal Seed Establishment, 1913

Hibbert Archives

Life changed considerably at Craig-y-Nos. All able-bodied men of a certain age were called up to serve their country. My grandfather was now fifty years old, so continued in his post of head gardener for Patti and Cederström. His team was depleted however, and even the baron pulled his weight, both in a manual and administrative capacity. A great effort was made by Con to produce more vegetables, and flower gardens were replaced by vegetable patches.

Patti's health was now cause for concern and between 1914 and 1917 she rarely left the castle, but she did visit London in 1917 to finalise her will. Virtually everything was left to the baron: cash estimated at $580,000, the Craig-y-Nos estate, stocks and bonds, plus all the household effects and jewellery. However she again demonstrated her considerable generosity towards her staff by leaving one year's wages to all the domestics who had been in service two years prior to her death. She left specific amounts to long serving senior members of her staff. My grandfather was bequeathed an amount which he never divulged, but having worked for her for 30 years, it was probably a reasonable sum as he was able to use it to build his retirement home.

It was clear Patti was affected greatly by the First World War. On her nineteenth wedding anniversary she wrote to Louise, her nephew Alfredo Barili's daughter, 'we will try and be happy if possible, which I doubt, as this war is absolutely finishing me slowly up'.

By the time the war finally ended, Patti's health had seriously worsened. In the following months she became weaker and weaker, with severe heart problems. On 27th September, 1919 she died peacefully at Craig-y-Nos. She was embalmed at Craig-y-Nos and laid to rest in her private chapel for nearly a month. During this time Con visited her daily with a fresh bunch of roses.

Her body was then taken to St Cynogs Church, Ystradgynlais, then on to the Roman Catholic church in Kensal Green, London, where the 'world' would pay their respects. She was finally buried, near Rossini, in Père-Lachaise Cemetery, in

TELEGRAMS
ABERCRAVE

Craig-y-Nos Castle,
Penycae, S.O.
Breconshire.

4th Dec 1920

This is to Certify that
C. Hibbert has been in
Baron Cederstroms' Service
as Head Gardener for
32 years. I can Thoroughly
recommend him as being
a reliable man, very
obliging & well up in his
duties, he is leaving as
the Baron has given up
his Establishment.

Will Heck.

agent

Con's reference, written by William Heck, Patti's agent

Paris. Baron Cederström would now put the castle up for sale. Con was retained at the castle for two years to help him with preparation for the sale, and to ensure the grounds were kept in prime condition.

The Winter Garden had been donated to the people of Swansea by Patti in 1918. After her death, arrangements were made to transport the building and erect it at the rear of Victoria Park, where it stands today as the Patti Pavilion. For Con it was an emotional farewell to the Winter Garden, which had consumed such a large amount of his life. He had nurtured and cherished it for nearly 30 years, since its inception in 1890. He also supervised the removal of Patti's large collection of tropical birds from her aviary at Craig-y-Nos to London Zoo.

Patti had invested her money wisely in the years before her death. The estate put up for sale was much larger than when it was purchased. It now consisted of 4 farms, a large working quarry with 33 acres of land, 17 cottages, and 23,000 acres of rough grazing. The estate, excluding the castle, went to auction at the Metropole Hotel Swansea on the 30th March, 1921. Only two farms were sold at that stage - Pentre Cribarth, opposite the castle, and once owned by Morgan Morgan, and Ongur Uchaf, off the road to Penwyllt.

The castle was sold privately in March, 1921 to the King Edward VII Welsh National Memorial Association for £19,000, to be converted into a TB hospital. At this time 'fresh air' was an important consideration for the cure of TB and Craig-y-Nos had an abundance of this. Streptomycin was discovered in 1944, and was the first specific anti-tuberculosis drug to be brought into clinical use. Con, who was now fifty-seven years old, applied to the new owners for employment. Prior to the sale of the Castle, Con had made sure he had the necessary reference to offer any prospective employer. He was to stay on as head gardener at the Adelina Patti Hospital until he retired on August 31st, 1933, at the age of sixty-nine. His career at Craig-y-Nos Castle had spanned 44 years.

In the meantime, my father Wilf had, at the age of thirteen, also started work at Craig-y-Nos. His main interest was the electricity generation plant at the castle: Patti had installed one of

Hibbert Archives

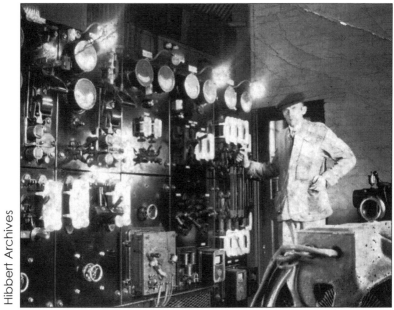

Wilf Hibbert in the electricity "Engine House" at Craig-y-Nos

Electricity Generation at Craig-y-Nos
Elwell Parker Dynamo, Marshall Compound Engine

Hibbert Archives

the first domestic systems in the UK. In the years that followed, my father became extremely knowledgeable in all areas of electrical engineering. He was very practical, and was completely self taught – mainly from the book *Modern Electric Wiring* by H H Cowley, published around 1928 and still in the family! His interests extended to the 'wireless' as it was introduced to the local residents. Our house was always cluttered with old radio sets and boxes of valves. The locals used the electricity charging facilities at Craig-y-Nos for their lead acid batteries - whether this was with hospital approval or not, I am not sure!

With the introduction of mains electricity in the upper Swansea Valley, in about 1949, he put his knowledge to good use, and was in great demand for wiring many farms and houses in the area. As a boy I remember accompanying him on many a visit to local farms to complete wiring projects in cowsheds, barns and stables.

The opening of Adelina Patti Hospital in the 1920s saw another community change in the Craig-y-Nos area. There was a need for trained nurses and young girls were encouraged to enrol. My mother, Getta Hibbert, and her sister, Sally Matthews, came from a Llansawel farm in Carmarthenshire to train as TB nurses in their late teens. The training was thorough and pretty tough, under the strict management of Matron Evans and later Matron Knox-Thomas. The medical procedures were harsh and cure rates fairly low. Much has been written of late about the severe treatment received by patients. What is clear is that a large number of very dedicated doctors and nurses, some with young families, risked their lives to give the best available treatment at the time, trying to cure as many patients as possible from the deadly illness. To this day my mother remembers well the emphasis placed on cleanliness in the hospital, and can still recall the regime followed to achieve this. Beds were moved every morning so that skirtings and walls could be disinfected. Staff ate exactly the same food as the patients; fresh vegetables, locally grown, and always a roast dinner on a daily basis. Nurses were trained how to serve the food in a proper manner, again with great care taken over cleanliness of plates. Dr Ivor Williams would regularly carry out spot checks on food being served.

Hibbert Archives

Nurses outside main entrance to Adelina Patti Hospital, 1950's

Nurse Getta Hibbert, left, with patient and another nurse

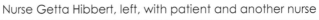

Hibbert Archives

Getta Hibbert left Craig-y-Nos in 1963 to pursue a career with Glamorgan County Council and was appointed matron of a home for the aged in Caerphilly. When she was fifty she attended a course at the Newport and Monmouth College of Technology on Residential Social Work. I recently discovered an essay she wrote whilst studying at the college and in it she recalls her time at Craig-y-Nos Hospital:

It was at this hospital that I commenced my training as a nurse, 36 years ago. During that time I witnessed many changes. The hospital accommodated 126 patients, male and female, adults and children. Tuberculosis was one of the principal scourges which afflicted the world. Medical science concentrated upon the task of eradicating it by understanding the varied forms of the disease. The main treatment was absolute rest, sometimes by immobilization of the patient in a plaster bed, some for six months, longer or less, depending on the extent of the disease and the period necessary for the diseased tissues to heal. Some patients would not respond to the rest, the disease would spread rapidly and deaths were not uncommon. The majority of the patients were young, of happy disposition, very attractive, with flawless peach-bloom complexion. Although most patients were on strict bed rest, the atmosphere in the wards was bubbling over. In the children's ward the majority were restrained in their cots, but it did not prevent the noisy playground atmosphere prevailing.

We all enjoyed the period of duty on the children's ward, we would get very attached to the babies, and found it very hard to say farewell when they became fit for discharge. I wonder if they gained that sense of trust in us, and what effect this long stay in hospital had on their development of personality.

During the Second World War, medical science progressed and produced an antibiotic drug, derived from mould, called streptomycin. A course of this drug was given to the patient in the form of intramuscular injection, the result being complete recovery for nearly all patients within a short period of time. The use of

Gwen, left, and Con with a friend at the bungalow

Con in his 'retirement garden' circa 1940

*this drug, with improved social conditions, visits to clinics, better
nutrition and public education meant a rapid decline in the disease:
the number of patients admitted to hospital became fewer.
At this time there was an urgent need for another type of hospital
in the area, somewhere to house and nurse the aged chronic sick.
The Adelina Patti Hospital was therefore converted into a geriatric
hospital. The building was not suitable, although gradually the
interiors of some of the established wards were converted and
upgraded. The atmosphere of some wards, with cancer, hemiplegia
and senility patients was one of confusion instead of happiness.
Perfumed wards with young patients looking forward to a long life
now had the very sick, the majority with a very short time to live.*

*The duties of the nurses became harder, but with little or no
result. Some of the young nurses left for more interesting and
fruitful work. We, the older nurses remained. Some of these
patients I knew when they were younger, healthy and ambulant.
In the process of ageing they had developed various problems. We
soon discovered the best treatment was a combination of kindness,
love, understanding, good food and cleanliness. Some would show
marked improvement, becoming less confused and even trying to
express their feelings of appreciation. This was very rewarding
and staff gained great satisfaction from the work.*

Both my parents worked at Craig-y-Nos Hospital, where
they met, and were married in 1937. The Second World War
was imminent, and food was becoming scarce. Craig-y-Nos
came under enemy fire, and a large bomb was dropped in the
field next to the castle. Unsuccessful attempts were made to
bomb the valley water supply at Cray, and Dan-yr-ogof caves
were used to store explosives. My parents told a story about my
eldest sister Gwenllian having to enter Swansea Hospital for an
operation. On one occasion when they visited her, the hospital
had been severely damaged by bombs and there was no sign
of my sister. Thankfully she had been moved to Langland Bay
and was safe.

Glyntawe School circa 1946 with headmaster Ithel Llewellyn, left

Glyntawe School march through Ystradgynlais, 1951 Festival of Britain

Con Hibbert and his wife Gwen had lived for 40 years in the gardener's cottage at Craig-y-Nos. Retirement for Con meant that he would have to seek other accommodation. His love of gardening meant that he would ideally have liked a large plot of land to continue his passion for cultivation. Around 1930 he purchased one third of an acre in a field opposite Craig-y-Nos Castle, part of Nant-y-gwared Farm. It was an elevated plot with grand views towards Craig-y-Rhiwarth and the Cribarth. He set about building a new bungalow, Craig-y-Nos Bungalow, which he and Gwen occupied until they both died in 1954. In 1951 Con and Gwen Hibbert celebrated 60 eventful and happy years of marriage, and a party was held at Craig-y-Nos Bungalow.

In 1953 at the age of 88 years Con was approached by the BBC for assistance in writing a script for a one and a half hour radio play about Adelina Patti, called the *Queen of Song*. A soprano, Marion Lowe, played the part of Patti, with Guy De Monceau as Nicolini and Eric Lugg as Con.

The play introduced Patti as a young girl of seven singing in New York and Signor Patti explaining how she was born on stage during a performance by Signora Patti in Madrid. It describes her first opera performance at the age of sixteen, and how she set sail for London in 1861 and sang the first four performances at Covent Garden unpaid!

She was a great success and her reign had begun. She moved on to conquer Berlin, Brussels, Amsterdam, The Hague and Paris, and then married the Marquis de Caux at the age of twenty-five, against the wishes of her father. The marriage, of course, ended in failure, Paris was besieged, and the Second Empire, along with with aristocrat de Caux lay in ruins. Patti was safe singing at Covent Garden with her future second husband, Nicolini. After several successful performances with Nicolini the play moves to the 'imitation Gothic castle' Patti and Nicolini bought in Wales. The narrator comments:

They knew nothing of the life of the natives. It meant nothing to them that as their crystal-clear river flowed to the sea it got steadily filthier, more fouled and ochred by the effluents of a hundred copper works, tin

Hibbert Archives

The last passenger steam train at Penwyllt, 1962

works and mines. Nor were they aware of the teeming masses that lived in the cramped, huddled, and narrow streets of Neath and Swansea. She realized their warmheartedness and began to repay them more and more by a wonderful generosity to various good causes and to people in need. In order to help the charities of South Wales, she sang for nothing.

It was encouraging to see that the script writers recognized the incredible charity work she did for the community. The play moves on to cover her American tours and her marriage to Nicolini.

The remainder of the play is located at Craig-y-Nos Castle, with the opening of the theatre, and Nicolini's love of fishing and shooting. There was an episode where Nicolini was shooting at birds as he was returning from the the mountain to the castle, and hit the conservatory window. Dai, the gamekeeper, exclaims, 'Jawch! He's peppered the glass. Oh, darro, if he's hit her.' The play mourns Nicolini's death at Pau in France, where he was taking the waters, but Patti was soon married again to Cederström. The wedding party is a fine affair on board a special train to London. The play concludes with her series of farewell tours and charity concerts before her health deteriorated, leading to her death in 1919.

As her embalmed body lay at rest in her own chapel at the castle, Con who had been with her for over 30 years, brought flowers to lay beside her. The play ends as follows:

Con Hibbert:	*Fresh flowers for M'Lady.*
Woman servant:	*I will take them*
Con Hibbert:	*Let me, please.*
Woman servant:	*You've brought roses again! Why don't you bring some gardenias? There are some, aren't there?*
Con Hibbert:	*M'Lady never did like gardenias near her, nor wallflowers, for that matter. And if it was lilac-time, I wouldn't bring lilac either. She didn't like it. I wish it was the time for violets: she loved those better than anything. Yes, I've brought her roses again. They're the last ones.*

The theatre at Craig-y-Nos today

The Patti Pavilion in its current home in Swansea

The play was broadcast on the evening of 23rd September,1953. I remember the BBC staff visiting my grandfather regularly for several months, and after transmission, he proudly showed me the box of cigars he received from the BBC for his efforts.

Con Hibbert died in Morriston Hospital on 14th February, 1954, at the age of eighty-nine. Gwen died seven months later, at the age of eighty-two. Con had lived in Craig-y-Nos for 64 years, 44 years as head gardener at the castle. His devotion to Patti and Craig-y-Nos, and its grounds, was unparalleled. His contribution to the development and maintenance of the gardens in Patti's reign, and subsequently for The Adelina Patti Hospital, was a true testimony to his skill and loyalty. He demanded high standards but was respected by his staff, and was a true gentleman. His admiration for Patti was clearly demonstrated by his wish that one of his granddaughters would be named after her. Con was eighty-three when my sister, Sarah Patti Hibbert, was born: he was a very happy man.

The post war period in Craig-y-Nos was a happy time for the local children. Most of the local children lived on farms and those that didn't, like myself,spent most of their spare time helping on the farms. Up until the 1950s, horses pulled all the farm implements. There was a day off from school on sheep shearing day and one only remembers the sunny summers and haymaking, particularly with the horses. Simple but enjoyable pleasures included horse riding, walking to Llyn-y-fan Fawr, winberry picking all day on the old Trecastle road, harvesting hazelnuts near Dan-yr-ogof Caves in autumn, and storing them for Christmas.

November 5th always meant a great celebration of fireworks at the hospital. A large bonfire would be built below the terraces facing the Tawe. This was an important event in the Craig-y-Nos calendar when all the local children were invited to attend and view the spectacle, from the balconies, alongside the young patients. A gentleman from Abercrave contributed a substantial amount of money annually towards this event.

There were one or two families with televisions in the 1950s, although the only television we saw up until about 1960 was on our visits to the hospital on a Sunday evening.

*To the memory of my old friends Con
and Gwen Hibbert and David Price*

The lark will rise o'er Llyn-y-fan, the place we loved so well,
On the wonders of one lonely dawn no more our lips will dwell,
And never more we'll wander in Twyni's narrow dell,
But while Tawe sings his song for me, dear friends,
I'll remember.

I'll remember how we laughed the golden hours of youth away,
How it seemed that stars and moonlight and happiness held sway,
When the nights that were filled with music followed a carefree day,
While Tawe sings his song for me, dear friends,
I'll remember.

I'll remember lovely Craig-y-Nos, wet with sun warmed April
showers,
That only fell to bring to birth a garden full of flowers;
How we gathered honeysuckle from Pen-twyn's leafy bowers,
While Tawe sings his song for me, dear friends,
I'll remember.

I'll remember when the Fan you loved wears its snowy crest,
When the hills are crowned with glory as sunset paints the West;
I'll remember when the Spring awakes in the valley where you rest,
While Tawe sings his song for me, dear friends,
I'll remember.

Ethel Rosate Lunn

The hub of all major activities was Glyntawe School and Callwen Church. Christmas time was a special occasion at the school. Every Christmas Day in the evening, all the excited children from the parish, including Penwyllt, congregated at Glyntawe school to welcome Santa and receive a gift.

Christmas was also a special time for the young patients of Adelina Patti Hospital. Santa used to visit all the wards on Christmas morning distributing his gifts. I went on more than one occasion to the children's ward and saw the joy this brought the sick children. My father was on both the school and hospital committees at different times, when there would be day long 'secret' expeditions to Swansea to buy the Christmas presents.

The Rev Bonsall Edwards and his wife worked extremely hard leading up to the Christmas festivities. There was the annual nativity play, and local children performed on two evenings in Callwen Church. This meant at least two rehearsals a week in the months of November and December. I remember on two occasions we were asked to perform at the Patti Theatre, Craig-y-Nos, for the patients. It was a great occasion – a proper stage and curtain. The performances were a huge success and Mrs Williams, Dr Ivor Williams' wife, treated all the cast to ice-cream cake!

One of the great pleasures of sitting in the garden on a summer's evening looking at Craig-yr-Rhiwarth, was to see in the distance, near Penwyllt, the smoke rising from the steam train as it pulled away from Penwyllt Station on its journey to Brecon, around 7pm every evening. It was a sad day in 1962 when the passenger services on this line were suspended, never to be again. One of my regrets is that I didn't make the journey on this train to Brecon from Penwyllt. I did travel on the Neath-Penwyllt section. The track has now been lifted and many of the road bridges demolished: a tourist opportunity well and truly missed!

The two main industries in Penwyllt thrived in the early years of the twentieth century, but around 1930 the demand for silica bricks was in decline, and the market was highly competitive. Production of bricks at Penwyllt was very labour intensive and when the owner of Kidwelly Brickworks, Sir Alfred Stephens, purchased the assets, it appears the future of brick production was uncertain. In 1926 a conveyance was made between Baron Cederström and Craig-y-Nos Silica Brick Company, set up by Sir Alfred Stephens. By 1933 it was known as the Penwyllt Silica Brick Company. Production of bricks at Penwyllt was wound down, and whereas in its prime more than 200 people were employed, by 1940 the works was closed and the few remaining employees were transferred with the brick moulds to the Kidwelly plant.

The limestone kilns continued production until their final closure in 1959. The outbreak of war in 1939, the policy for increased production of home grown food, and the requirements of the steel industry meant there was big demand for burnt lime. Burnt lime continued as a 'fertiliser' for many years after the war. I remember the lime spreaders passing our house each day on their way to the farms of Breconshire and beyond. From 1936 the limestone business was run by Jim Morris and his family, but eventually the need for burnt lime for use in agriculture was replaced by chemical fertilisers. From 1959 to 1963 the quarry lay dormant, but as the demand for limestone aggregate for roadmaking increased, production of limestone at Penwyllt was resumed. The quarry was taken over by Hobbs, and later by Wimpey Hobbs, but it has now ceased operation.

Few properties are now occupied in Penwyllt. Powell Street is the headquarters of the South Wales Caving Club. The remains of the kilns and brickworks are to be seen clearly, and the Stump Inn is still standing but not occupied. Glyntawe School was no longer needed and is now used as the Dulwich College Field Centre.

The Adelina Patti Hospital finally closed as a hospital in the early 1980s, and in 1986 was put up for sale by the Secretary of State for Wales. The rest of the grounds had been the responsibility of the Brecon Beacons National Park Authority since 1976. The castle was sold to Mr Cecil Jones in 1988, and for 8 years he made a determined effort to repair and maintain a building which, by now, was in a very bad state. The theatre continued to be used for occasional performances by local operatic societies. From 1995 to 2000 the castle was owned by Dr & Mrs Trevor Jones, who continued with its refurbishment.

In 1996 the renowned Welsh soprano, Dame Gwyneth Jones, planned to establish a trust, with the intention of developing the castle as a teaching establishment for professional opera and other music, the theatre and grounds providing a magnificent setting. Unfortunately it seems that funding was a major issue, and the plan did not materialize. The castle was sold to its current owners in 2000.

There is no doubt that the last 200 years have been interesting times for the upper Swansea Valley: the discovery and production of a wide range of minerals; the establishment of communities; the demise of thriving industries; the influx of workers from around the globe; the glamour and wealth of the most famous diva of her generation, Adelina Patti, making a permanent home at Craig-y-Nos.

Her contribution to the Swansea Valley must never be underestimated. Patti, who lived at Craig-y-Nos for 41 years, was not only a worldwide opera star, but very much a part of the community. Her great affection for the local people was shown by her generosity to those less fortunate than herself. William Terriss, an actor deputizing for an indisposed Henry Irving at the grand opening of the Patti Theatre in 1891, described her perfectly:

Our gracious and gifted hostess, the chatelaine of Craig-y-Nos. The good fairy who haunts the 'Rock of the Night'. The true friend of the poor, whose benefactions have for a dozen years past ripened unnumbered throughout the length and breadth of this picturesque region.

My wish is to see the Patti Theatre, this beautiful Grade 1 listed building, restored to its former glory, to be used for the benefit of the local community and for the development of talented young singers, actors and musicians. Planners need to be resolute to ensure the original structure of both the theatre and castle retain their integrity - as close to the original design as possible. The gardens should be improved, to once again reflect some of their past beauty, and a monument erected in the castle grounds to finally recognize what Adelina Patti did for the community in this part of Wales.

Bibliography

The Reign of Patti, H Klein, 1920

Queen of Hearts, J F Clone, 1993

Queen of Song, BBC Radio Play, 1953

Ongur Uchaf Farm and its Occupiers, S Barrows & D Downey, 1993

Madam Patti and Craig-y-Nos Castle, D S Downey, 1992

My Recollections of Madame Patti, E Rosate-Lunn

A History of the County of Brecknock, T Jones, 1898

Adelina Patti and Craig-y-Nos, Canon J Jones-Davies

The Victorian Country House, M Girouard, 1971

Craig-y-Nos Castle, Gardeners Chronicle, 1882

Brecon and Radnor Express 1899

The Brecon Forest Tramroads, S Hughes and P Reynolds, 1990

Craig-y-Nos, Gwenllian Hibbert,Y Fesen

The Great Forest of Brecknock, J Lloyd, 2008

A Topographical Dictionary of Wales, S Lewis, 1849

Fineleaf